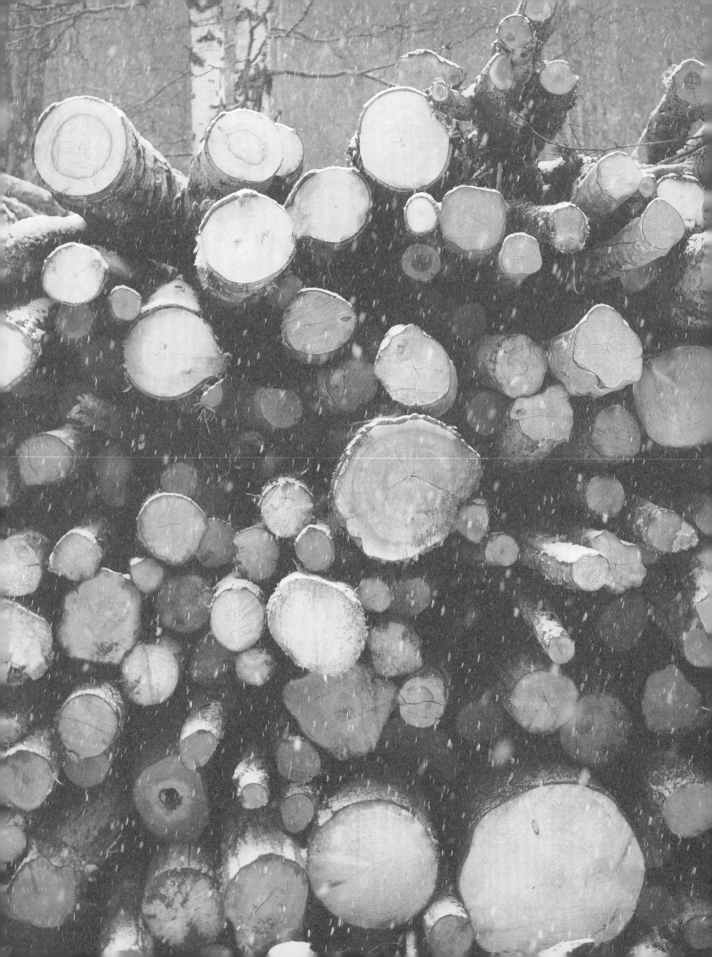

North

WILD

KITCHEN

Home Cooking *from the* Heart *of* Norway

North
— WILD —
KITCHEN

Nevada Berg

PRESTEL
MUNICH · LONDON · NEW YORK

Contents

Introduction

The aged timber creaks beneath my feet, as a gentle breeze seeps through the small crevices in the log walls. I lower my head as I make my way inside our seventeenth-century *stabbur*. The stabbur, a traditional storage house for food, was once a necessity for many farms across Norway. Before refrigeration, fish and livestock were cured and hung to dry, while other goods, such as flour and flatbread, were kept here as well. This stabbur is just one of many dotted across the country, especially throughout the area of Numedal, the great medieval valley I now call home.

Not long ago, I arrived in Norway, with my Norwegian husband and son, after years of nomadic travel. Longing for a home and community to be rooted in, we came to an unexpected place. A place deep in the belly of Norway, where the mountains tower and a river storms through a winding valley. Then we did something many young people seem to do these days when they move to the countryside: We bought a farm—a mountain farm. We bought it before I had ever seen it in person. This lovely, old farm tells the stories of those who came before us, and bears witness to a part of Norway's traditional food culture.

I knew before I came to live here that there was so much more to Norwegian food than I was aware of—more than just the contrast of meat and boiled potatoes versus the New Nordic cuisine, which finds chefs presenting local food in a technical yet aesthetically beautiful way that is not easy to replicate at home. But I was still surprised to find the vast amount and incredible quality of the produce and livestock available, and to discover that deep in the northern wild, lies one of nature's culinary banquets. Seasonal, forgiving, abundant—like a land flowing with milk and honey.

My understanding of Norwegian cuisine went from an unfortunate stereotype to a world filled with berry-infused moose sausage, fermented trout, wild nettle soup, rhubarb juice made from birch sap, home-brewed beer, and traditional cheeses and porridges made on the farm. The variation and quality of the dishes struck something deep inside me and I found myself asking why the bounty and complexity inherent in the Norwegian kitchen was not more well known, not to mention more commonly praised and highlighted.

As I started to explore the cuisine, I had the privilege to meet the people behind the local products. People who are intensely passionate about maintaining their family traditions and creating new ones. They even inspired me to make my own variations using local ingredients. I started writing about everything I was learning—cataloging recipes, stories, and traditions—and I wanted to share my excitement with everyone, so a few months after we arrived, I started my blog, *North Wild Kitchen*. I also picked my first wild European blueberry that year, and salted and hung to dry my first leg of lamb. We raised nineteen chicks to provide a steady flow of fresh, free-range eggs and I picked, canned, and froze far too many plums. Even now, with every passing moment, the list continues to grow.

The more I study and read about Norway's food culture, the more I grasp its simultaneous simplicity and complexity. It's simple in that traditionally most Norwegians used what they had available, making everyday dishes for sustenance rather than for pleasure or creativity. At the same time, Norway has a rich and complex culinary heritage that's deeply influenced by other Scandinavian and European countries. Religion and wealth distribution throughout the centuries, as well as geography and social and cultural differences, also played a role in the eating habits of Norwegians. For instance, while the wealthy enjoyed exotic imported ingredients, the majority of the population, who were poor to say the least, used a few basic ingredients to make hearty meals to fill the belly and provide fuel for a hard day's work. The landscape also affected the diet, from the coast and fjords to the mountains and lowlands. Settlements often isolated people, which led to national dishes taking on slight differences from region to region, so that one dish could have more than a hundred variations. It's a cuisine that has evolved, and continues to do so, while also holding on to many of its traditions.

This cookbook is more than just a collection of Norwegian dishes. It is an exploration of the where, the why, and the how—the history and stories beyond the plate. There are traditional recipes that have been passed down for centuries, as well as newer recipes that are so embedded in the food culture that it seems like they've been traditional Norwegian dishes all along. I also include recipes that utilize Norwegian ingredients in creative and innovative ways. Together, these create a more complete and accurate picture of Norwegian cuisine and how Norwegians eat today.

I hope you'll journey with me as I examine some of the most iconic symbols and activities related to Norway's food and culinary traditions, and expand upon them with corresponding recipes. I've tried to share dishes that can be translated across countries, and to use ingredients that can be substituted to fit what's available to you. This is just a small collection of recipes, representing what I've been exposed to thus far, and is in no way an exhaustive collection. This is more of a beginning, a scratch on the surface of what Norway offers. I hope this broadens your definition of Norwegian cuisine, while also providing a glimpse into the many exciting ingredients this country has to offer. I also hope it inspires you to look at the ingredients in your own surroundings and to be creative and experimental in your own kitchen.

Norwegian Cuisine Today

To define what is authentic Norwegian cuisine is to accept the overlaps and influences created by centuries of trade and migration and the adoption of culinary dishes from other regions and cultures. Understandably, Norway shares many similarities with its Nordic neighbors, as well as mainland Europe and the northernmost parts of the British Isles. The country has also been exposed to food from other parts of the globe, opening its diet to new flavors and popular dishes from near and far.

Norwegian cuisine still features many traditional dishes, but the modern palate reflects a more worldly perspective that enjoys a range of international products and dining experiences, such as tapas and wine bars. Pizza and tacos are the norm, with Friday being deemed "Taco Friday," while takeout options like kebab and sushi are popular late-night meals. Trends also

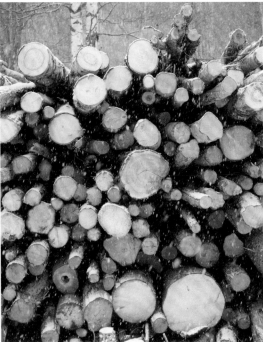

dominate the culinary scene, with food trucks popping up and restaurants serving the latest culinary craze. And yet, behind the grandeur and excitement of the new, there's still a strong interest in learning traditional techniques and using local ingredients.

Chefs are putting their marks on Norwegian ingredients and traditions, and revolutionizing the way the cuisine is perceived. At the same time, artisans and craftsmen are utilizing what's available to them locally, and making a name for themselves and their products both domestically and internationally. Fish and seafood remain one of the country's most important exports—and the quality is recognized around the world—but Norway now boasts some of the best cheesemakers in the world. There's also a focus on sustainability and using the country's incredible natural ingredients in a responsible way. Best of all, this excitement and innovation is filtering throughout the country and more Norwegians are being drawn to cooking and gaining a fresh perspective on the cuisine.

From the past, we can take valuable lessons in cooking methods, such as smoking, preserving, and storing, as well as hunting. Survival encouraged time-tested processes that we're returning to now, so we can learn from them and also remember what a fish that's cooked on a stone over a hot fire in the middle of the forest tastes like. And as we are blessed to live in abundance and have a knowledge of and access to food and methods from around the globe, we can integrate both the past and the present into innovative and inspired meals, all the while taking advantage of the incredible bounty. By every definition, these meals are Norwegian, because the products are locally sourced, and the tastes embody the evolution of the Nordic plate.

Notes on Ingredients and Equipment

The idea behind each recipe is to highlight Norwegian ingredients, but if you're unable to access these ingredients or equipment, substitutions are heartily welcome. Innovation in the kitchen happens when we are inspired to try making new things with what we have.

It's also important to note that the outcome of any dish reflects the quality of the ingredients used. An apple plucked straight from a tree branch will taste much different than one flown in and sold in a grocery store.

Ingredient measurements are listed in both imperial and metric measurements. In some instances, they are rounded up or down to match more closely with each other and make it easier for you, independent of which measurement system you use. These slight differences should not affect the outcome of the recipes.

BUTTER—Common Norwegian butter tends to be lightly salted and I use this butter in all my baking and cooking. Some recipes contain margarine because this is how the recipe was passed down from generation to generation. If you wish to omit the margarine, substitute it with lightly salted butter.

CHEESE—I often refer to white cheeses made of goat's milk, which are not to be confused with soft fresh goat cheese. These are usually semi-firm and have a mellow goat flavor.

CULTURED MILK—I use *kulturmelk* and kefir, products of soured milk, in cheesemaking and baking. For the recipes in this book where I normally use kulturmelk, I have listed buttermilk in the ingredient list. For the recipes using kefir, it's also fine to substitute with buttermilk.

DAIRY—Norwegian dairy products contain high percentages of fat. Full-fat sour cream, for example, is 35 percent fat. I specify which recipes require full-fat dairy products; elsewhere you can use lower fat products.

EGGS—My eggs come straight from our hens and I always leave them at room temperature. When possible, use room temperature eggs.

FLOUR (BARLEY, RYE, WHOLE WHEAT)—In Norway, barley, rye, and whole-wheat flours come in both fine and coarse textures. Fine flours are similar in texture to all-purpose flour whereas coarse flours, sometimes referred to as stone ground, have a rougher texture. If coarse flours are not readily available, try specialty bread shops or a local baker.

FLOUR (WHITE)—When it comes to white flour, I use all-purpose flour, sifted. However, it's not necessary to use sifted flour for non-baking recipes and I have specified this in those recipes. For a gluten-free option, substitute equal parts sifted GF flour.

FRUIT AND BERRIES—Many of the fruits and berries we use are grown in our garden or picked in the wild. Here are substitutions for those that might be harder to access:

Bilberries (European blueberries)—blueberries

Blackcurrants—blackberries (although, they taste completely different)

Cloudberries—golden raspberries

Lingonberries—cranberries

OIL—I use good-quality rapeseed oil in the majority of my cooking and baking. In all of the recipes calling for oil, I have suggested you use a mild-flavored oil, like canola or a mild olive oil, since rapeseed oil might not be readily available in your area.

MEATS—I'm a firm believer in using high-quality meat, preferably sourced locally from a farmer or butcher.

SUGAR—I always use granulated sugar unless specified in the recipe.

SYRUPS—In Norway, there are two kinds of syrup, light and dark. The closest substitute for light syrup is golden syrup, which you should be able to find in specialty shops. For dark syrup, substitute with light molasses.

WILD MEATS—Use the following guidelines for substitutions:

Venison (deer)—moose, reindeer (caribou), and elk are interchangeable

Pheasant—chicken or turkey

Moose—elk or venison

Grouse—partridge or quail

Hare—chicken or turkey

Beef, lamb, or goat can also be used as substitutes for any of these wild meats, but the flavor profiles will be drastically different.

RICER—This kitchen accessory is helpful for getting a smooth consistency from the potatoes used to make flatbreads and *lefse*. I highly recommend investing in one.

ROLLING PINS—Norwegians use various indented rolling pins to make lefse and flatbreads. I have tested all the recipes with a regular rolling pin as well, and it works fine, though it takes a little extra effort.

TAKKE—This Norwegian griddle is very large, round, and can be electric or heated by fire. If you can't access one, use a frying pan instead. You won't be able to cook as many cakes or breads at once, or make them as large, but they'll turn out great nonetheless.

Sankingen

THE FORAGE

Foraging is a unique expression of connectivity. Since ancient times, people have gathered food from nature to provide sustenance and energy. Today, foraging is one of life's pleasures, and for Norwegians, a way to combine fresh air, exercise, and a good meal following a successful pick.

The day is unstructured, with open expectations. You follow the curves of the landscape and the rays of the sun. The sounds of branches crackling underneath, streams trickling nearby, and leaves dancing in the breeze all become part of the day's soundtrack. Foraging is about more than the edibles themselves; it's about the moments, the laughter, the stillness, and the discovery. It's as much about the journey as the destination, and fosters a deeper connection to nature and ourselves.

There is something romantic about eating what nature provides, especially when you've never given it such thought before. When we take the time to look a bit closer, we inevitably discover. What may have seemed like an obtrusive bed of weeds—or perhaps an overly lush landscape—becomes an array of edibles in varying tastes and textures. And with their bounty of vitamins, minerals, and nutrients, they're a welcome relief after a long, barren winter.

Norway's incredible array of wild edibles has left a distinct mark on the cuisine. Wild berries, such as bilberries, lingonberries, strawberries, and cloud-berries are showcased in dishes throughout the summer and autumn months. Hundreds of wild mushrooms, such as chanterelles and hen of the woods, appear in late summer. Juniper and its berries have long been used as a flavor enhance-ment, as well as a means for producing homemade beer. Wild herbs and plants like dill, caraway, parsnip, angelica, wild garlic, chervil, and horseradish have been documented as popular ingredients dating back to the Viking age and possi-bly even earlier. Stinging nettle, tree sap, and wild flowers make delectable drinks, among other things. Along the coasts, you'll find sea kale, pepperwort, scurvy grass, and sea rocket complementing the various fish and seafood found in the sea. And this is just a tiny sample of the local, ecological, healthy, and free foods available throughout the Norwegian landscape.

Understanding what's accessible right in front of us is powerful. It celebrates the nuances of ingredients in their native environment, and opens the doors to endless culinary adventures. Putting nature on the menu has become more enticing and popular these days, thanks in part to gourmet kitchens, the New Nordic movement, and our desire for a more sustainable and direct approach to our food system. Going out and picking for oneself and then experimenting in the kitchen encourages an adventurous spirit, and provides the freedom to cook in a way that makes food more than just a meal; it becomes a lifestyle.

In Norway, we have the concept of *allemannsretten* ("every man's right"), which is the right to use nature freely, independent of who owns the property. Included in this tradition is the right to travel the land, stay on the land, and gather from the land. The main rule is to be careful and respectful of nature, as well as the people who own the land and those who will come after. People are free to pluck wild plants, flowers, bushes, and mushrooms. Wild nuts must be eaten on location, and collecting tree sap requires permission from the landowner.

The unwritten agreement is to take only what you need. This idea—it's a way of life, really—reflects Norwegians' respect for nature. Fulfillment comes not only from taking what we need, but also from ensuring that we leave something for others to enjoy as well. This, in turn, allows nature to replenish itself, and helps create a sustainable cycle.

In this chapter, I touch briefly on some of the more common edibles foraged in Norway and those that are most easily recognized and accessible. With any foraging expedition, it is extremely important to be one hundred percent sure that what you are picking is indeed fit for consumption and not dangerous. Some edibles can look like poisonous variations, so always seek out the help of local experts and take caution.

Wild Garlic Soup

RAMSLØKSUPPE

Wild garlic, or ramps, can be found along the coasts and in the forests of Norway, mainly in May and June. The season is short, only a few weeks, and as quickly as this delightful plant grows, it withers before the start of summer. Wild garlic is a culinary treasure, used by chefs and home cooks that want to serve up the perfect taste of springtime. It's also incredibly nutritious, and has been valued for centuries for its medicinal properties.

With its subtle garlic flavor, this delicate green is incredibly versatile, and makes a nice addition to soups, salads, tarts, and sauces. It's one of those ingredients that requires only a little imagination to go a long way in the kitchen. If you can't get your hands on wild garlic, substitute garlic chives. • *serves 4*

2 tablespoons lightly salted butter
1 medium onion, finely chopped
3 medium potatoes, peeled and diced
4¼ cups (1 l) vegetable stock

7 ounces (200 g) wild garlic leaves, roughly chopped
Salt and pepper
Heavy cream (optional)

In a large, heavy saucepan, heat the butter over medium heat. Add the onion and sauté for 8 to 10 minutes or until soft and translucent. Add the potatoes and sauté for about 5 minutes to soften them slightly, stirring often. Add the vegetable stock and bring to a boil. Lower the heat and simmer, covered, for 15 to 20 minutes or until the potatoes are cooked all the way through. Add the wild garlic leaves and cook for 2 to 3 minutes or until the leaves have wilted. Transfer to a blender, or use an immersion blender, and purée until smooth, being careful of the heat. Season to taste with salt and pepper.

Serve in individual bowls with a dash of heavy cream on top, if using.

Creamy Sorrel Potato Salad

POTETSALAT MED ENGSYRE

———————

Sorrel, known as *engsyre* or *surblad* ("sour leaves") in Norwegian, arrives in early spring and stays until late fall. It's a hearty herb and comes back every year, which means there will always be a supply on hand to use. Sorrel has a crisp and tangy bite to it, almost like a sour apple, making it an ideal herb to brighten up dishes like salads and fish.

Potato salad is a common side dish in Norway and throughout the Nordic region. The classic version is mayonnaise-based and features spring onions. With the addition of radishes and hard-boiled eggs, plus sorrel dominating the dressing, this is definitely a spin on tradition. I tend to favor extra dressing with this salad, so the sorrel really stands out against the egg and potatoes. *serves 4*

5 medium non-starchy potatoes, such as new potatoes, rinsed	1 ounce (28 g) young sorrel leaves, plus more for garnish
½ cup (120 ml) mayonnaise	½ teaspoon salt
½ cup (120 ml) sour cream	4 to 5 radishes, thinly sliced
½ teaspoon strong mustard	3 large hard-boiled eggs, chopped

In a large pot, cover the potatoes with cold salted water and bring to a boil. Lower the heat and simmer for 10 to 15 minutes, until the potatoes are barely tender when pierced with a knife. Drain the potatoes and return to the pot. Cover with a tea towel and let rest for 15 minutes. Peel the potatoes and cut into bite-size pieces.

While the potatoes are cooking, combine the mayonnaise, sour cream, mustard, sorrel, and salt in a food processor and pulse until the sorrel is fully incorporated into the dressing.

In a large serving bowl, combine the potatoes, radishes, and hard-boiled eggs. Add the sorrel dressing, gently toss, garnish with more sorrel leaves, and serve.

Beer-Battered Spruce Tips with Syrup

GRANSKUDD FRITERT I ØL MED GRANSKUDDSIRUP

Toward the end of spruce tip season in the late spring, the tips lengthen and their citrus aspect intensifies, making them ideal for battering and frying until golden brown. You get a lovely lemon taste with a chewy yet soft texture. These are delicious right out of the oil with a little salt, but turn into something extraordinary when dipped into spruce tip syrup. It's a balance of sweet and savory, with floral and citrus notes. Feel free to substitute with the tips from other edible conifers. *serves 4*

FOR THE SPRUCE TIP SYRUP

4 to 5 handfuls spruce tips

About 2 ½ to 3 cups (500 to 600 g) granulated sugar

FOR THE BEER BATTER

1 cup (240 ml) ale or lager

1 cup (120 g) all-purpose flour, sifted

½ teaspoon salt

FOR THE SPRUCE TIPS

4 cups (960 ml) cooking oil

2 to 3 handfuls 2-inch-long (5 cm) mature spruce tips

Flaky salt

For the spruce tip syrup, in a medium saucepan, combine the spruce tips and just enough cold water to barely cover and bring to a boil. Lower the heat and simmer, covered, for 30 minutes to extract the flavor. Pour through a mesh strainer into a large, heavy saucepan; discard the spruce tips. Measure the liquid and calculate 2 parts sugar for every 3 parts liquid. Combine the calculated sugar and liquid in the large, heavy saucepan and bring to a boil. Continue boiling, removing any white foam that forms on top, until reduced and thickened to the point when the syrup coats the back of a spoon. For accuracy, use a candy thermometer and remove the syrup from the heat when it reaches the thread stage (230°F / 110°C). Place in a clean glass jar with a lid and let cool.

For the beer batter, in a medium bowl, whisk together the beer, flour, and salt. Let rest for 15 minutes.

While the batter is resting, heat the cooking oil in a medium, heavy saucepan over medium-high heat. When you can drop in a little batter and it begins to sizzle, the oil is hot enough.

Line a large plate with paper towels.

For the spruce tips, dip the tips in the batter, making sure they are evenly coated. When the oil is hot, carefully place 2 to 3 tips in the oil and fry, turning once, for about 1 minute, or until crisp, golden brown, and cooked through. Transfer to the paper towel–lined plate and immediately sprinkle with flaky salt. Repeat with the remaining spruce tips.

Serve immediately with the spruce tip syrup on the side.

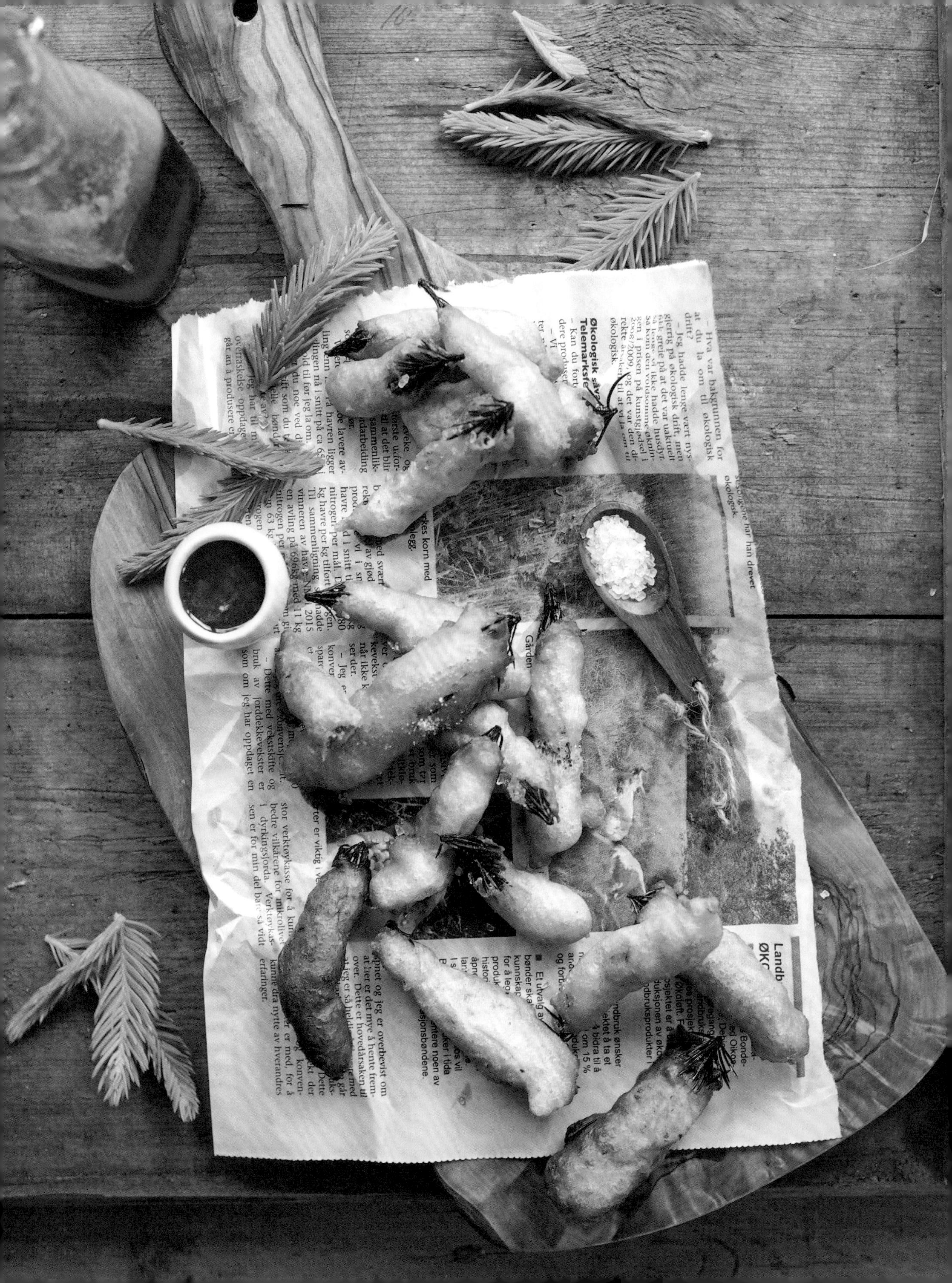

Oatmeal with Raw Spruce Tip Granola and Blackberries

HAVREGRØT MED GRANSKUDDGRANOLA OG BJØRNEBÆR

Late in spring, Norway's luscious spruce trees start to change. Fresh shoots with brown casings appear, and as the days pass, the casings break open and small, vibrant green tips begin to emerge. The little shoots continue to grow and fan out, eventually blending in and turning into dark green needles. It can be easy to miss the change, but in those few short weeks when the tips are sprouting, you can gather them and use them in a variety of dishes and drinks. The tips are full of vitamin C and have a lovely citrus taste. Young tips tend to be more flavorful and less acidic, so it's good to pick them right when they are just budding.

Porridge maintains an important place in Norwegian culinary culture. Here, I've combined fresh spruce tips with nuts and blackberries to give this hearty dish an earthy flavor profile reminiscent of the mountains. Be sure to use whole milk for wonderfully rich and creamy oatmeal. *serves 4*

2 cups (200 g) quick-cooking oats

4 cups (960 ml) whole milk

½ teaspoon salt

2 tablespoons whole, raw almonds, unsalted

2 tablespoons whole, raw hazelnuts, unsalted

2 tablespoons sunflower seeds, unsalted

2 tablespoons pumpkin seeds, unsalted

6 tablespoons freshly picked spruce tips

2 tablespoons granulated sugar

1 cup (125 g) blackberries

In a medium, heavy saucepan, combine the oats, milk, and salt and bring to a boil, stirring frequently. Lower the heat and simmer for about 5 minutes or until the oats are soft, continuing to stir.

Combine the almonds, hazelnuts, sunflower seeds, pumpkin seeds, spruce tips, and sugar in a food processor and pulse until blended but still chunky.

Divide the warm oatmeal among bowls, top with the raw granola and blackberries, and serve.

Wild Nettle and Honey Cake

BRENNESLEKAKE

———————

Sprouts of stinging nettles pop up in late spring and within a few short days, they begin their swift and relentless siege to take over the ground. While known for their dominance and sting, with good gloves and boiling water, nettles can be handled and tamed. They've long been appreciated for their medicinal and health benefits, as well as for their texture and culinary potential. Even the Vikings understood their value; nettle fibers were discovered in the Oseberg find, a Norwegian Viking burial ship from around 834 AD.

This subtly sweet cake is a great introduction to nettles, as they pair incredibly well with honey. And it will impress everyone, especially when you reveal that the star ingredient is that prickly weed growing in the yard. · *serves 10 to 12*

FOR THE CAKE

2 big handfuls young nettle leaves, washed

½ cup (112 g) lightly salted butter, softened

1 cup plus 2 tablespoons (220 g) granulated sugar

3 large eggs, at room temperature

½ cup (120 ml) honey

2½ cups (300 g) all-purpose flour, sifted

2 teaspoons baking soda

FOR THE WHIPPED CREAM

2 cups (480 ml) heavy cream

2 tablespoons granulated sugar

½ teaspoon almond extract

Preheat the oven to 300°F (150°C). Butter 2 (8-inch / 20-cm) round cake pans and line with parchment paper.

For the cake, bring a medium saucepan of water to a boil. Add the nettle leaves, lower the heat, and simmer for about 5 minutes. Drain the nettles, transfer to a blender or food processor, and purée until smooth. Set aside to cool.

In a large bowl, use an electric mixer to beat the butter and sugar until fluffy. Add the eggs, 1 at a time, incorporating each egg before adding the next one, and continue beating for a few minutes until thick, creamy, and light yellow. Add the honey and nettle purée and beat until thoroughly blended.

In a medium bowl, whisk together the flour and baking soda. Add to the butter mixture and beat until combined—it will be slightly stiff. Pour the batter into the prepared pans and bake for 30 to 35 minutes or until a toothpick inserted in the center of the cake comes out clean. Let the cakes cool in the pans for 10 minutes before turning them out onto a wire rack. Let cool completely.

For the whipped cream, whip the heavy cream, sugar, and almond extract until stiff peaks form.

To assemble the cake, spread some of the whipped cream on top of 1 cake. Place the other cake on top and spread the rest of the whipped cream on the top and, if you like, on the sides. Refrigerate until ready to serve.

Mini Nettle Pavlovas

BRENNESLEPAVLOVA

———————

Although it has roots elsewhere, Pavlova has a prominent place in Norwegian baking. It's even one of the most searched for recipes in the country, especially for Constitution Day on May 17th. To put a "foraging" spin on traditional Pavlova, I've added stinging nettles. The taste is sensational, with the mild earthiness of the nettles balanced against the sweetness of the Pavlova. We have wild raspberries growing nearby, so I like to pick some for this recipe. • *makes 12 Pavlovas*

FOR THE NETTLE POWDER

2 to 3 big handfuls young nettle leaves, washed

FOR THE PAVLOVAS

4 large egg whites, at room temperature

¾ cup (150 g) granulated sugar

1½ teaspoons cornstarch

FOR THE SYRUP

1 cup (200 g) granulated sugar

1 cup (240 ml) water

2 handfuls young nettle leaves, washed

FOR THE WHIPPED CREAM

1½ cups (360 ml) heavy cream

¼ cup (30 g) confectioners' sugar

Raspberries, for serving

Preheat the oven to 375°F (190°C).

For the nettle powder, spread the nettles on a baking sheet and bake for 12 to 15 minutes or until dry. Let cool then transfer to a food processor and pulse until powdery but still flaky. Set aside.

Lower the oven to 215°F (100°C). Line a baking sheet with parchment paper.

For the Pavlovas, in a large bowl, use an electric mixer on medium to whip the egg whites until foamy. Gradually add the granulated sugar, whipping until stiff peaks form. Add the cornstarch and 1½ tablespoons of the nettle powder and use a spatula to gently fold until combined. Using a spoon, form the mixture into 12 small (4-inch / 10-cm) nests on the prepared baking sheet then press a slight indentation in the center of each. Bake for 1½ hours or until firm and dry on the outside, but still light in color. Cool on a wire rack.

For the syrup, in a medium, heavy saucepan, combine the granulated sugar and water and bring to a boil. When the sugar has dissolved, remove from the heat and add the nettles. Let steep for about 3 minutes then strain through a mesh strainer, reserving the syrup and discarding the nettles. Return the syrup to the saucepan and simmer over medium heat until just thickened. Be careful not to simmer too long; the liquid may harden. Set aside to cool.

For the whipped cream, whip the heavy cream and confectioners' sugar until stiff peaks form.

Place a dollop of whipped cream on top of each Pavlova, sprinkle with raspberries, drizzle with syrup, garnish with more nettle powder, and serve immediately.

Wild Strawberry Soup with Wild Field Mint Cream

MARKJORDBÆRSUPPE MED ÅKERMYNTEKREM

———————

There's nothing quite like strawberries, especially Norwegian strawberries, to mark the start of summer. They're highly prized, as the cooler climate allows the berries to ripen much slower, developing a sweeter and more intense taste. *Markjordbær*, the smaller and even more sought after wild strawberries, start to appear around this time, making them an excellent berry to use in one of the most refreshing and simple desserts of the season, fruit soup.

Since wild strawberries can be difficult to get ahold of, you can use cultivated berries—the soup will still be delicious. I like to add whipped cream infused with wild field mint (*mentha arvensis*), but you can use whatever mint you have on hand. Just be sure to adjust for the strength of the mint, as some mint has a stronger flavor and won't need to infuse as long. • *serves 4 to 6*

FOR THE MINT WHIPPED CREAM

1 cup (240 ml) heavy cream

¼ cup (2 g) fresh wild field mint leaves, plus more for garnish

1 teaspoon granulated sugar

FOR THE STRAWBERRY SOUP

1 cup (240 ml) water

5 tablespoons (60 g) granulated sugar

18 ounces (510 g) wild strawberries

1 tablespoon freshly squeezed lemon juice

For the mint whipped cream, place the heavy cream in a clean glass jar with a lid. Tear the mint leaves and stir into the cream. Seal the lid and refrigerate overnight.

Strain the cream through a mesh strainer into a medium bowl and discard the mint. Add the sugar and whip until just firm, so the cream has a smooth and velvety texture—it should keep its shape but also melt into the soup when stirred. Refrigerate until ready to use.

For the soup, in a medium, heavy pot, combine the water and sugar and bring to a boil. When the sugar has dissolved, add the berries and lower the heat. Cover and very gently simmer for about 5 minutes or until the berries are soft and falling apart. If using cultivated strawberries, this will take longer, about 30 minutes. Remove from the heat and cool slightly. Stir in the lemon juice then purée in a blender or with an immersion blender until smooth. Cover and refrigerate until completely cool.

Divide the soup among bowls, top with the whipped cream, garnish with chopped mint, and serve immediately.

Cloudberry Caramels with Sea Salt

MULTEKARAMELLER

These intriguing caramels feature Norway's cloudberries, which are also known as golden berries, and grow briefly and sparingly in the mountains. They're also nicknamed *fjellets gull* ("mountain's gold") for their color, and because finding them is like discovering hidden treasure. Cloudberries can be difficult to find, so try experimenting with other berries, such as yellow raspberries.

makes about 36 caramels

10½ ounces (300 g) fresh cloudberries

1 cup (240 ml) heavy cream

4 tablespoons (60 g) lightly salted butter

1¼ cups (250 g) granulated sugar

¼ cup (60 ml) Norwegian light syrup or golden syrup

¼ cup (60 ml) water

½ teaspoon vanilla extract

Flaky sea salt

In a medium saucepan, bring the cloudberries to a low simmer to soften them and release their juices. Pour the berries into a mesh strainer set over a bowl and press the berries through to extract as much juice as possible. Discard the seeds. Measure ½ cup (120 ml) purée and set aside. Reserve the rest for another use.

Line an 8 × 8-inch (20 × 20 cm) baking pan with parchment paper, leaving a 1-inch (2.5 cm) overhang on all sides. Butter the parchment paper.

In a small, heavy saucepan, heat the heavy cream and butter over medium heat until the butter melts. Remove from the heat and stir in the reserved ½ cup (120 ml) cloudberry purée.

In a large, heavy pot, gently heat the sugar, golden syrup, and water over medium heat. Use a heatproof rubber spatula to wipe down the sides of the pan and prevent sugar crystals forming. Clip a candy thermometer to the side of the pot, raise the heat to medium high, and bring to a boil without stirring. Once the mixture reaches 250°F (120°C), remove from the heat.

Gradually and carefully pour the cloudberry mixture into the hot sugar mixture—it will bubble up vigorously—and gently stir with a heatproof rubber spatula until fully combined. Place the pot back over medium-high heat and continue cooking until the mixture reaches 240°F to 245°F (116°C to 118°C). Remove from the heat and quickly whisk in the vanilla. Pour the mixture into the prepared pan and let sit at room temperature for at least 3 hours or until the caramels are set.

Use the parchment paper to lift the caramels from the pan and place on a cutting board. Use a very sharp knife to cut into approximately 1-inch (2.5 cm) squares then sprinkle with the sea salt. Store the caramels, wrapped individually in wax paper, in an airtight container, for up to 3 weeks or freeze for up to 6 months.

Creamy Chanterelle and Goat Cheese Skillet

KANTARELLER MED HVIT GEITOST

————

They say the forests of Norway are full of gold during late summer and early autumn, when mushrooms can be found by anyone who looks. Chanterelles, which are practically worth their weight in gold, have a bright yellow hue and curved caps, so they nearly give themselves away against the mossy forest bed.

You might find yourself on a *sopptur*, or "mushroom hunt," to find these delicacies growing all over the mountainous regions of Norway. These hunts are one of life's little pleasures and one of the many ways Norwegians combine fresh air, exercise, and a delicious hand-picked feast.

I like to cap off a successful mushroom hunt by cooking this simple, one-pan dish over an open fire. It's rich and creamy, and will keep any belly satisfied while the main meal slowly cooks away. Toast some bread on the grill and pass it around the campfire for dipping into the gooey mixture. • *serves 4 to 6*

1 tablespoon lightly salted butter

2 to 3 handfuls chanterelles (enough to evenly fill the skillet), halved if large

A few sprigs fresh thyme

Salt and pepper

¾ cup plus 1 tablespoon (200 ml) heavy cream

1 pound (450 g) semi-hard goat's milk cheese or another melting cheese, grated

1 loaf white bread, cubed and grilled

Preheat a large cast-iron skillet on a grill secured over a prepared open fire. Add the butter and once it begins to foam, add the chanterelles. Toss in some of the sprigs of thyme, season to taste with salt and pepper, and sauté for 8 to 10 minutes or until the chanterelles are barely tender. Move the pan to a part of the grill where the heat is lower. Add the heavy cream and cook, stirring often, until the mixture thickens a bit. Add the grated cheese and let it melt, without stirring, then carefully remove from the heat.

Sprinkle with more thyme and serve immediately with grilled bread for dipping.

Homemade Bilberry Cordial

BLÅBÆRSAFT

Cordials have been a part of the Norwegian table for centuries and continue to be made at home. They're one of many ways to preserve the plentiful vitamins and nutrients packed into berries, and ensure a steady supply throughout winter.

One of my favorite cordials is made with wild bilberries, which are also known as European blueberries; they have a subtle flavor but deep color. As soon as we walk out our door, we're surrounded by bilberry bushes, so picking them becomes an affair, with everyone grabbing a bucket. We eat as we go along, and when we return with our bounty, our fingers and lips are stained with the fruits of our labor. If you can't access bilberries, substitute other blueberries. *makes about 3 cups (720 ml)*

¾ cup plus 1 tablespoon (200 ml) water

2¼ pounds (1 kg) fresh bilberries or other blueberries

2½ to 3 cups (300 to 400 g) granulated sugar, plus more as needed

In a heavy pot that's large enough to fit the berries, bring the water to a boil over high heat. Lower the heat slightly, add the berries, and cover. Cook, stirring no more than once or twice to keep the berries intact, for 10 minutes or until the berries have softened and released their juices.

Pour the berries into a cheesecloth-lined mesh strainer set over a large saucepan and let stand for at least 30 minutes, without pressing on the berries.

When the berries have finished straining, measure the strained juice and pour it into a clean heavy pot. Add the required amount of sugar—2 cups (400 g) for every 4¼ cups (1 l) juice—and bring to a boil. Lower the heat and simmer while stirring for 5 minutes or until the sugar has dissolved. Taste and add more sugar, as needed.

Carefully transfer the cordial to a clean glass bottle (or bottles), cover with a lid, and let cool. Store the cordial in the refrigerator for up to 2 weeks.

To serve, pour a little bit of cordial into a glass and add water to taste.

Juniper Beer

EINERØL

Brewing beer is a time-honored tradition in Norway, and holds a central place in Nordic culture. Weaker beer was enjoyed during the day, while stronger brews, made with the best grains, were saved for special occasions. In the Middle Ages, farmers were required to make beer for Christmas; otherwise, they'd face fines and if they failed to produce beer for three consecutive years, they'd risk losing their land.

Juniper was one of the most important ingredients in traditional Norwegian home brewing. It's even quite possible that juniper was the main brewing herb, with hops replacing it sometime after the Middle Ages. Before the introduction of sugar to Norway, juniper also provided beer's sweetness and because it contains very little sugar, the beer had very little alcohol. Sugar is a modern addition, though in this recipe, the alcohol content is still quite weak.

There are many variations of juniper beer, with some using whole branches and others using only the berries. Different species of juniper will provide different tastes, so experiment with what you find. Be sure to correctly identify the species before brewing, as some juniper is toxic. For this recipe you'll need basic brewing equipment, such as a fermenting bucket, bottles, bottlecaps, and a capper, all of which must be sterilized beforehand. Accuracy is especially important when brewing beer, so I recommend weighing all the ingredients, even the liquid ones. *makes about 25 (12-ounce/355-ml) or 18 (17-ounce/500-ml) bottles*

2 ⅔ gallons (10 l) water

Enough juniper branches with berries to fill a large pot

¾ ounce (20 g) hop pellets, such as Columbus/Tomahawk/Zeus (CTZ) pellets

14 ounces (400 g) Norwegian dark syrup or light molasses

1 cup (200 g) dark brown sugar, packed

¾ ounce (20 g) brewer's yeast

Be sure to sterilize all brewing equipment before beginning.

In a large, heavy pot, combine the water, juniper branches, and hop pellets and bring to a boil. Lower the heat, cover, and gently simmer for 20 minutes. Using sterilized tongs, remove the branches then strain the mixture through a mesh strainer into a large sterilized container, such as a fermenting bucket. Add the dark syrup and brown sugar and stir until well blended. Cool to 90°F (32°C).

Dissolve the brewer's yeast in a little warm water then add it to the cooled mixture. Cover and let stand in a warm spot for 2 days. Bottle the beer, using sterilized bottles, then store in a cool, dark place for at least 1 week and preferably 2 weeks to give the flavors a chance to mellow before consuming.

Rowanberry and Apple Chutney
with Hazelnut Bread

HASSELNØTTBRØD MED ROGNEBÆR- OG EPLECHUTNEY

———————

This recipe is a delicious way to enjoy some of autumn's best wild edibles—bitter rowanberries, sweet apples, and fragrant hazelnuts. Serving the chutney on a slice of hazelnut bread with a slice of sharp cheese makes it an excellent appetizer or snack. If you have access to wild apples, use them instead of cultivated ones. · *makes 2¼ cups (540 ml) chutney and 1 small loaf of bread*

FOR THE CHUTNEY

6 small apples, preferably a tart and firm variety, peeled and diced

4½ ounces (125 g) fresh rowanberries

1 medium onion, finely chopped

½ cup (100 g) granulated sugar

3 tablespoons apple cider vinegar

1 teaspoon freshly grated ginger

½ teaspoon salt

FOR THE HAZELNUT BREAD

2 cups (240 g) all-purpose flour, sifted

½ cup (60 g) fine whole-wheat flour

½ cup (60 g) coarse whole-wheat flour

1 teaspoon active dry yeast

1 teaspoon rapeseed oil

1 teaspoon honey

1 teaspoon salt

1 cup (240 ml) water

⅔ cup (70 g) whole hazelnuts, skins on, roughly chopped

Sharp cheese, for serving

Fresh wild herbs, such as sorrel, for serving

For the chutney, in a medium, heavy saucepan, combine the apples, rowanberries, onion, sugar, apple cider vinegar, ginger, and salt and bring to a boil. Lower the heat and gently simmer, uncovered and stirring occasionally, for 20 to 30 minutes or until the berries are soft and the liquid is significantly reduced. Let cool then cover and refrigerate up to 2 weeks.

For the bread, in a stand mixer fitted with the dough hook, combine the all-purpose flour, fine and coarse whole-wheat flours, yeast, rapeseed oil, honey, salt, and water. Knead for 15 minutes or until the dough is smooth and elastic. Alternatively, knead the mixture by hand.

On a floured surface, press the dough into a rough square, large enough to sprinkle the hazelnuts over the surface of the dough. Fold the dough over and briefly knead the dough to distribute the nuts then shape it into a ball. Place the dough in a lightly oiled bowl, cover with a tea towel, and let rise in a warm place for 2 hours or until doubled in size.

Preheat the oven to 475°F (240°C).

Arrange the dough on a parchment paper–lined baking sheet, sprinkle with a little flour, and let rise in a warm spot for 45 minutes.

Place the bread on the bottom rack of the oven and immediately lower the temperature to 400°F (200°C). Bake for 40 minutes or until golden brown. Let the bread cool completely.

Slice the bread and top with a slice or two of sharp cheese, followed by some chutney. Garnish with wild herbs and serve.

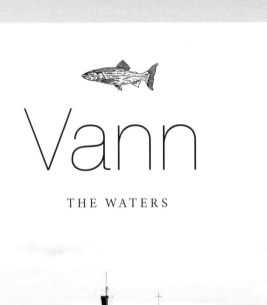

Vann

THE WATERS

The waters carve through the landscape, etching an

elaborate pattern of flowing streams, gushing waterfalls, and still lakes. They surround the edges of the country, extending their depths beyond the horizon. To separate the waters from the land is impossible, as these two elements are intertwined in a natural harmony. After all, Norway is a land of water.

Water provides beauty, and balances Norway's rocky yet lush terrain. It's also a source of trade, travel, and exploration. It offers an abundance of food, which has long sustained the population, while also providing a means of commerce. As a result, Norway has a distinct relationship with and a deep respect for its waters and what lies beneath.

Archeological surveys reveal fishing was conducted in Norway's seas, rivers, and lakes during the Stone Age, and possibly earlier, with fish being a critical resource for those living along the coast. During the eleventh century, fish was traded as a domestic good, while in the twelfth century, Norway began exporting dried cod and herring to England. During the thirteenth century, the German Hanseatic League and its trade organizations established themselves in Bergen, a city on Norway's southwestern coast. They soon took control of the dry fishery trade in northern Norway, and continued to dominate the industry for nearly four hundred years.

Cod and herring have long been the most important stocks exploited by Norwegian fisheries. If you travel along the western coast moving north, you can still see wooden structures perched along the cliffs and draped with rows and rows of cod, laying exposed and vulnerable to the forces of nature. Favorable climatic conditions are essential in the processing of *tørrfisk* (dried cod) and *klippfisk* (salted and dried cod), the oldest and largest fish exports, though this process occurs more typically indoors now. The natural elements dry out the fish, but it can be brought back to life with just a simple soak in water. It's a fascinating cycle, in which fish is formed in the water then transformed by the sun and wind and ultimately returned to the water to become something new.

To store an abundance of fish without using much salt or other preservatives, fishermen in the Middle Ages used a fermentation technique that involved wrapping oily fish in tree bark and burying it in sand to keep it cold. While this specific technique is no longer used—it can actually be quite dangerous—salting and fermenting is still practiced in Norway, and the result is a delicacy known as *rakfisk*. And then there's gravlax (or *gravlaks* in Norwegian), one of the most widely recognized dishes in the world, and another example of fish preserved in salt.

Fishing continues to dominate the region, with Norway being the second largest exporter of fish and seafood in the world. For Norwegians, fishing is an activity that brings you into nature, providing a satisfying meal wrapped around a memorable experience. It's also easily accessible. Salmon, trout, perch, and pike are popular catches for those wishing to cast their line in rivers and lakes, while heading along the coast delivers lobster, king crab, mussels, clams, cod, mackerel, and urchins, to name just a few.

Norway's emphasis on interacting with nature in a sustainable and nurturing way has resulted in the incredible preservation of fish and seafood in their natural environment. This, in turn, provides products that are arguably the best in the world. When you hear stories from local fisherman and divers, you begin to fully comprehend how deeply connected Norwegian culture is to its natural bounty. And when you taste those ingredients, you appreciate that connection even more.

In this chapter, I include some of Norway's more popular fish and seafood dishes, but this doesn't even begin to scratch the surface of the vast diversity found in the country's waters. If possible, I encourage you to source fish and seafood yourself, or to visit a local fishmonger who can provide the freshest ingredients possible.

Gravlax with Mustard Sauce
and Dill-Stewed Potatoes

GRAVLAKS

Gravlax is made up of the Scandinavian words *grav* and *laks*, which translate to "buried salmon." In the Middle Ages, fisherman buried the fish in sand and within a few days, it would ferment and resemble its closest modern-day relative, *rakfisk*.

Gravlax, much to the relief of many, has evolved, and is now made in a process that involves curing the fish in a salt and sugar mixture under refrigeration. The result is an orange-pink, dill-infused delicacy. It's simple to make at home and the taste is extraordinary. My Norwegian family always serves gravlax with dill-stewed potatoes and their favorite mustard sauce.

I recommend using frozen fish, as freezing eliminates any trace of bacteria or parasites. Allow the fish to defrost in the refrigerator for about twelve hours before starting. Having it almost but not entirely thawed makes it easier to fillet. If using fresh fish, make sure it's as fresh as possible. This recipe can also be used with trout. • *serves 6 to 8*

FOR THE GRAVLAX

About 6¾ pounds (3 kg) whole fresh or frozen salmon or trout

Granulated sugar: use 5 tablespoons (75 g) per 2¼ pounds (1 kg) fish

Fine salt: use 5 tablespoons (75 g) per 2¼ pounds (1 kg) fish

20 black peppercorns, crushed

2 to 3 bunches fresh dill, chopped

FOR THE MUSTARD SAUCE

¾ cup (180 ml) mayonnaise

2 tablespoons whole-grain honey mustard

2 tablespoons heavy cream

Dash of orange juice

2 teaspoons finely chopped fresh dill

FOR THE POTATOES

6 medium waxy potatoes, peeled

2 cups plus 1 tablespoon (500 ml) milk

3 tablespoons lightly salted butter

2 tablespoons all-purpose flour, sifted

Pinch of nutmeg (optional)

Salt and pepper

1 bunch fresh dill, finely chopped

For the gravlax, fillet the fish so you have 2 large skin-on fillets; remove the bones. I recommend checking for bones again when the curing process is complete.

In a large bowl, combine the sugar, salt, and peppercorns. Spread about ⅓ of the mixture in an even layer on the bottom of a roasting pan, top with about ⅓ of the dill, and place a fillet, skin-side down, on top. Spread about ⅓ of the salt mixture and ⅓ of the dill on the flesh side of the fillet then arrange the second fillet, flesh-side down, on top. This way the skin is on the outside and the flesh sides are pressing against each other. Spread the remaining salt mixture and dill on the skin side of the top fillet, discarding any excess. Cover the fillets with a cutting board or wood plank

and top with something that weighs 2¼ to 4½ pounds (1 to 2 kg). Refrigerate for 2 days. Every 12 hours, turn the fish fillets over without separating them and pour any juices in the pan over the top and sides of the fillets. After 2 days, take the fillets apart and pat them dry. Wrap the fillets together in aluminum foil and refrigerate for 1 more day to enhance the flavor. The gravlax is ready to be served at this point or can be refrigerated for up to 5 days or frozen for up to 3 months.

For the mustard sauce, in a small bowl, whisk together the mayonnaise, mustard, heavy cream, orange juice, and dill. Cover and refrigerate for up to 1 week.

For the potatoes, in a large pot, cover the potatoes with cold salted water and bring to a boil. Lower the heat and simmer for 15 minutes or until the potatoes are barely tender when pierced with a knife. Drain the potatoes and cool slightly. Cut the potatoes into small cubes.

In a small saucepan, heat the milk until warm; cover and keep warm.

In a heavy, large saucepan, heat the butter over medium-high heat. Add the flour and cook, stirring, for 2 minutes without browning. Slowly add the warm milk, whisking constantly, then lower the heat to a gentle simmer. Add the nutmeg and season to taste with salt and pepper. Continue cooking, whisking constantly, for about 5 minutes or until the sauce is thick. Add the potatoes and cook, stirring gently, for 2 minutes or until warmed through. Stir in the dill.

Slice the gravlax into thin strips and serve with the mustard sauce and dill-stewed potatoes.

Hot-Smoked Mackerel

VARMRØKT MAKRELL

———————

Summer brings an abundance of mackerel to the coastal areas. Considered natural "citizens" of the Norwegian coastline, they migrate up the coast to follow krill, a type of small crustacean that gives mackerel its incredible taste.

Mackerel is an extremely important resource for southern Norway and its arrival is met with much joy and anticipation, especially in the city of Kristiansand. Interestingly, mackerel was traditionally only consumed in eastern and southern Norway, because, while not at all accurate, there used to be a superstition in the north that mackerel ate corpses at the bottom of the sea.

Superstitions aside, fresh mackerel is fantastic and hot-smoking is one of the best ways to prepare it, as it gives the fish delightfully deep flavor, and turns its distinctive striped and shiny skin an incredible golden hue. Hot-smoked mackerel is typically served as finger food. • *serves 4*

Wood chips, such as alder or birch, for smoking

4 to 8 fresh mackerels, depending upon the size

Coarse salt

Soak the wood chips in a bowl of cool or lukewarm water for 1 hour.

Prepare the mackerel by cutting off the heads and gutting and cleaning the fish. Rinse under cold water and pat dry. Liberally salt the fish, inside and outside, and let stand at room temperature for 30 to 45 minutes. Rinse off the salt with cold water and pat dry.

If using a charcoal grill, heat the coals on one side and place a foil tray filled halfway with water on the opposite side, under the grill rack. Once the coals are hot, place a handful of the water-soaked wood chips on top of the coals. Arrange the grill rack over the coals and water tray then place the mackerel on the rack, directly over the water tray. If using a smoker, follow the manufacturer's setup instructions and arrange the wood chips, water, and mackerel accordingly. Close the grill or smoker, open the vent directly above the mackerel, and smoke for about 40 minutes or until the meat is falling from the bones.

Arrange it on a serving plate, with sour cream, sliced red onions, and flatbread alongside, and invite everyone to dig in with their hands.

Creamy Fish Soup

KREMET FISKESUPPE

There's nothing quite like sitting on the docks enjoying a warm bowl of creamy fish soup with the sound of the waves coming in and the seagulls singing in the distance. Variations abound across the country, but perhaps the most well-known fish soup comes from Bergen. It's thick with fish and shrimp, speckled with carrot, celery, and onion, and seasoned with a little vinegar and sugar. I like my soup teeming with fish and vegetables and with a velvety broth that draws you right to the water's edge. Feel free to vary the mix of fish and seafood to your liking, adding in mussels or even leftover fish cakes or fish balls. • *serves 4*

4 tablespoons (60 g) lightly salted butter

1 onion, chopped

1 fennel bulb, trimmed and cut into very thin, short strips

1 medium carrot, peeled and cut into very thin, short strips

1 small leek, washed and thinly sliced

½ large red bell pepper, cut into very thin, short strips

4¼ cups (1 l) fish stock

9 ounces (255 g) boneless salmon fillets, cut into pieces

9 ounces (255 g) boneless cod fillets, cut into pieces

9 ounces (255 g) shrimp (optional)

1 cup (240 ml) heavy cream

Juice of ½ lemon

Salt and pepper

Finely chopped fresh flat-leaf parsley leaves, for serving

In a large, heavy pot, heat the butter over medium-high heat. Add the onion and sauté for 5 minutes or until soft and translucent. Add the fennel, carrot, leek, and bell pepper and sauté for 2 minutes. Add the fish stock and cook for 2 to 3 minutes or until the vegetables are softened but still firm. Add the salmon, cod, and shrimp, if using, and cook for 5 minutes or until cooked through. Add the heavy cream and lemon juice and season to taste with salt and pepper.

Divide the soup among bowls, sprinkle with the parsley, and serve immediately.

Simple Fish Cakes

FISKEKAKER

Fish cakes are one of the most popular and iconic fish dishes in Norway. For dinner, they're traditionally served with brown gravy and a side of boiled potatoes smothered in melted butter. Often, a quick lunch means buying a couple warm fish cakes and sandwiching them inside a crusty roll.

In my opinion, the best fish cakes are made at home. The classic version features a spongy patty with a smooth consistency and a hint of nutmeg, but there are more innovative takes as well. Everyone has their favorite approach, but as long as you highlight the fish, you really can't go wrong. My recipe was inspired by an Oslo-based fishmonger. They're simple yet flavorful thanks to the addition of onion. Using fresh fish is essential, as frozen won't bind into cakes.

makes 8 large cakes

½ large onion

1 pound (450 g) fresh pollock or haddock fillet, cut into pieces and checked for bones

1 teaspoon salt

1½ tablespoons potato starch

½ teaspoon ground white pepper

1 cup (240 ml) whole milk

Lightly salted butter, for frying

In a food processor, pulse the onion until finely chopped; transfer to a bowl and set aside. Place the fish and salt in the food processor and pulse for 30 seconds or until a rough paste forms. Add the potato starch, pepper, the chopped onions, and some of the milk and pulse to combine. With the food processor running, gradually add the rest of the milk then process 1 minute longer. The mixture should be wet yet firm with a spongy texture.

Use a large spoon dipped in warm water to scoop out some of the fish cake mixture then use your hands to shape it into a large patty. Repeat to create 8 patties total.

In a large, heavy frying pan, heat the butter over medium heat. Working in batches, add a few cakes to the pan and cook, flipping as needed, 3 minutes per side or until both sides are golden brown. To test the cakes, press on the center with your finger; it should be firm to the touch. Repeat with the remaining cakes and serve warm.

Dried and Salted Cod Stew

BACALAO

—————

While *bacalao* may not look or sound Norwegian, it has in every way become a part of the cuisine. Making *tørrfisk* ("dried cod") was a tradition for centuries, but in the sixteen hundreds, Norwegians began borrowing from other countries, and started salting cod before laying it on rocks to dry. This became an extremely important export, especially for the city of Kristiansund, which sent ship after ship of *klippfisk* ("salted and dried cod") to Spain. In the 1830s, Spanish ships began collecting the fish directly from Kristiansund to avoid higher taxes. This period is known as *spansketiden* ("the Spanish time"), and this dish is one of its lasting impacts.

Garlic is an uncommon ingredient in classic bacalao, because it was considered, at the time, to be unappealing to Norwegians due to its unpleasant smell and taste. Not to upset any purists, but I really like the addition of garlic, especially the way it infuses into the oil. • *serves 4 to 6*

2¼ pounds (1 kg) boneless salt cod

¾ cup (180 ml) olive oil

3 large cloves garlic, minced

3 small dried pequin peppers, crushed, or ½ teaspoon dried chili flakes

2 large onions, cut into rounds

2¼ pounds (1 kg) waxy potatoes, peeled and thinly sliced

2 (28-ounce / 800-g) cans chopped tomatoes

2 red bell peppers, sliced

¾ cup (180 g) tomato paste, mixed with 2 tablespoons water

Finely chopped fresh flat-leaf parsley, for serving

In a large pot, cover the cod with cold water and let stand for 24 to 36 hours, uncovered, changing the water twice during that time. Drain the fish and cut into 1½-inch (4 cm) pieces.

In a large, heavy pot, heat the olive oil over medium-high heat. Add the garlic and pequin peppers, using more or less to suit your taste, and sauté for 2 minutes or until the garlic starts to brown and the oil is fragrant. Remove half of the infused oil and set aside. In the same pot, begin layering, in this order, a third of the onions, potatoes, cod, tomatoes, bell peppers, and the reserved oil. Repeat the layering and overlapping twice with the remaining vegetables and oil. Pour the tomato paste and water mixture over the vegetables. The dish produces a lot of liquid, so don't worry if the tomato paste mixture seems thick at this point. Cover and bring to a boil. Lower the heat and simmer gently, shaking the pot occasionally but never stirring, for 1 hour or until the potatoes are barely tender when pierced with a knife.

Sprinkle with the parsley and, if desired, serve with olives and crusty white bread.

Beer-Steamed Mussels with Lovage

BLÅSKJELL DAMPET I ØL

Mussels are the most common shellfish found along the Norwegian coast, and though the best time of year to eat mussels is late autumn to the early spring, most people prefer the picturesque surroundings of a warm summer day by the water. There's no denying the feeling of sitting down to a bowl of mussels and a glass of white wine or a cold beer, with the sun shining on your face. They make a great appetizer or a complete meal, and take just minutes to pull together. I particularly like steaming mussels in good beer and adding lovage for more flavor. The taste and scent of lovage is similar to celery and parsley, but it's more aromatic, so a little goes a long way. Stirring butter into the sauce just before serving helps cut through any lingering bitterness from the beer. *serves 4*

4½ pounds (2 kg) mussels

6 tablespoons (84 g) lightly salted butter, divided

6 large shallots, sliced

6 cloves garlic, finely chopped

2 cups (480 ml) good-quality lager beer or ale

½ cup (12 g) lovage leaves, chopped, plus more for serving

Salt and pepper

Crusty bread, for serving

Rinse the mussels under cold water, scrubbing them with a brush. Discard any broken mussels and use your hands or scissors to pull off any hairy clumps (beards) along the shell openings.

In a large, heavy saucepan, heat 2 tablespoons of the butter over medium-high heat. Add the shallots and garlic and sauté for 2 minutes or until softened. Add the beer and bring to a boil. Add the mussels, cover, and cook for 5 to 8 minutes or until the mussels open. Using a slotted spoon, transfer the mussels to a large bowl, discarding any that didn't open. Add the lovage and the remaining 4 tablespoons butter to the liquid in the pot and simmer for 1 minute. Season to taste with salt and pepper.

Pour the liquid over the mussels, sprinkle with more lovage leaves and serve immediately with crusty bread alongside.

Fresh Boiled Crabs

KRABBE NATURELL

———

The very best crabs are caught in late September and early October, because after a long summer, they have more meat and roe. While crab is served in many ways, there is a long tradition of cooking freshly caught crab in seawater right on the docks. The result is firm, white meat that's sweet and tasty. It goes best with buttered white bread, mayonnaise, and lemon wedges.

Calculate 1 to 2 whole, live crabs
per person

Fill a heavy pot that is large enough to fit all the crabs with enough fresh seawater to just cover the crabs—don't put the crabs in the pot yet. If using fresh water, add in ¼ cup (50g) fine salt per 4¼ cups (1 l) water. Bring to a boil then add the crabs, making sure there's room between them. Cover and cook for 15 to 20 minutes or until the small claws can be easily pulled off. Using tongs, remove the crabs and let cool slightly.

Clean the crabs by first removing the abdomen on the underside of each crab. Remove the outer shells by lifting up firmly. Discard the stomach, guts, and the grey, feathery gills. Rinse the crabs thoroughly to ensure they're clean.

Serve the crab as is or with buttered white bread, a little mayonnaise, and lemon wedges. Have a nutcracker and small forks on hand for retrieving the meat. Cooked crab can be stored in an airtight container in the refrigerator for up to 2 days.

Fish and Mashed Potatoes with Roasted Carrots, Sautéed Leeks, and Bacon

PLUKKFISK

When we lived abroad, my husband always wanted to make this fish dish from Bergen, because he had such fond memories of it from home, but to me, it just seemed like fish and mashed potatoes. After all these years, I was determined to understand why *plukkfisk* is so beloved. I went to the source of my husband's plukkfisk addiction, my mother-in-law, who makes hers the way her grandmother did, with a lot of butter stirred into mashed potatoes. It's exceptional. I created my version with her suggestions in mind. I keep the dish relatively simple, and add the carrots, leeks, and bacon on top, rather than mixed in. Fat is essential to plukkfisk, so don't skimp on the butter and cream! • *serves 4*

FOR THE ROASTED CARROTS

4 carrots, peeled and cut lengthwise into quarters

Mild-flavored oil for roasting

Salt and pepper

FOR THE FISH AND POTATOES

1½ pounds (675 g) starchy potatoes, peeled and cut in half

3 tablespoons lightly salted butter, plus more for frying

½ cup (120 ml) milk

½ cup (120 ml) heavy cream

1 teaspoon salt

1 pound (450 g) boneless cod fillet

A couple slices bacon or other cured meat, chopped (optional)

2 leeks, washed and sliced

Fresh flat-leaf parsley, chopped, for serving

Preheat the oven to 400°F (200°C).

For the carrots, arrange them on a baking sheet, drizzle with the oil, season to taste with salt and pepper, and toss to coat. Bake for 15 minutes or until nicely browned and tender.

In a large pot, cover the potatoes with cold salted water and bring to a boil. Lower the heat and simmer for 15 minutes or until the potatoes are barely tender when pierced with a knife. Drain the potatoes and return to the pot. Add the 3 tablespoons butter, along with the milk, heavy cream, and salt and mash until creamy; the potatoes will thicken as they stand.

Fill a medium pot with cold salted water and bring to a boil. Add the cod, lower the heat, and simmer for 5 minutes or until cooked through but not falling apart. Drain and set aside to cool then break into small pieces and stir into the potatoes.

If using bacon, fry in a pan with a little butter until crispy. Remove from the pan and set aside. Add the leeks, and if not using bacon add more butter to the pan, and sauté for 3 minutes or until soft.

Divide the plukkfisk among bowls and top with the leeks, carrots, and bacon. Sprinkle with the parsley, top with more butter if you're feeling indulgent, and serve.

Lemony Baked Salmon with Cucumber Salad

OVNSBAKT LAKS MED AGURKSALAT

This is a quick, easy, and delicious meal. It's one of the first dishes I tasted while living in Norway, and has become a favorite staple I serve family and friends. Whenever I make it, the air fills with the aromas of baking salmon, butter, and lemon, which always brings a sense of comfort. You can use a whole salmon fillet or individual fillets, as I've done here. Served with cucumber salad, boiled potatoes, and sour cream (which you can serve with a little horseradish mixed in), it's a complete meal. • *serves 6 to 8*

FOR THE CUCUMBER SALAD

1¼ cups (300 ml) white vinegar

1¼ cups (300 ml) cold water

½ cup (100 g) granulated sugar

Pinch of salt

2 large English cucumbers, thinly sliced crosswise, or peeled into ribbons

FOR THE SALMON

8 salmon fillets with skin, about 2¼ pounds (1 kg) in total

4 tablespoons (60 g) lightly salted butter, cut into small pieces

1 large lemon, thinly sliced

1 teaspoon dried parsley

1 teaspoon salt

½ teaspoon pepper

Boiled potatoes and sour cream, for serving

For the cucumber salad, combine the vinegar, water, sugar, and salt in a large bowl. Add the cucumber slices and let stand at room temperature for 30 minutes. Don't leave the cucumbers any longer or they'll soften too much and lose their crisp.

Preheat the oven to 400°F (200°C).

For the salmon, place the fillets in a baking dish and arrange the butter and lemon in between and on the sides of each of fillet, sprinkling any leftover butter and lemon on top. Sprinkle with the parsley, salt, and pepper and bake for about 15 minutes or until the fish is opaque in the center.

Serve the salmon with the cucumber salad, as well as boiled potatoes and sour cream.

Smoked Trout Mousse

RØYKT ØRRETMOUSSE

In Numedal, where our farm is located, we have access to some of the best trout in Norway. When we make a big catch, we like to fry a couple right away, smoke a few fillets, and then freeze the rest for another day. Whenever I have leftover cold-smoked trout, I make this delightful mousse. It's so easy and yet it has enough sophistication to seem like it would require more work than it does. I typically serve this as an appetizer with flatbread, potato pancakes, crispy bread, or slices of boiled potato. It's also nice to take along on a short hike and serve with some crackers for a light lunch. • *serves 4*

½ pound (225 g) cold-smoked trout

½ cup (120 ml) heavy cream

4 ounces (113 g) cream cheese

Zest and juice of ½ lemon

Salt and pepper

1½ teaspoons chopped fresh chives, plus more for garnish

In a food processor, combine the trout, cream, cream cheese, and lemon juice. Pulse until creamy yet still slightly coarse. Transfer to a bowl and season to taste with salt and pepper. Gently incorporate the chives.

You can serve the mousse immediately, but the flavors are best if allowed to rest overnight in the refrigerator. Garnish the mousse with the lemon zest and more chives and serve as a dip or on top of flatbread, potato pancakes, sliced and boiled potatoes, crispy bread, or crackers.

Seteren

THE SUMMER MOUNTAIN FARM

The *seter* blends into nature, while it simultaneously
learns from it, protects it, nurtures it, and praises it. On these traditional mountain farms, the workload is heavy, but there's little—save possibly a radio, a good book, or a thoughtful conversation—to distract from the majesty and peacefulness of the landscape. The soundtrack is a harmonious blend of the bleating and lowing of animals, and the clanking of their bells as they move across the land.

Visiting a seter provides the quintessential Norwegian farm experience. These summer farms can be found spread across the country, in the valleys, the fjords and along the coast.

Typically a cluster of buildings, summer farms emerged as an extension of the farmhouse to utilize grazing areas not suitable for year-round habitation, and focus mostly on milk production from cows and goats. The practice of summer farming is said to be almost as old as farming itself—archaeological finds trace it back to the Iron Age in the seventh century—and still to this day it remains an integral part of the Norwegian agricultural system.

Why the seter method began in Norway is unclear, but theories suggest that as farms expanded, it became difficult for grazing animals to return to the farm on long summer evenings. There was no easy way to ensure animals would remain within property lines and herding them home every day was a daunting task. Also, utilizing the pasture opportunities of the surrounding mountains meant the feed at home could be reserved for winter. By the twelfth century, *Gulatingsloven*, or "old Norwegian law," stated that if a farmer failed to herd his animals on summer pasture, he could be reported for illegal grazing or "grass robbery."

Although it's easy to romanticize seter life, traditionally the days were long and filled with hard work. It was primarily women that lived and worked on the seter, with the children joining them. There was no electricity or running water, and the sleeping quarters were small and shared. Milking the cows and goats was a daily chore and the animals had to be herded often and kept within their respective boundaries to ensure they didn't wander into neighboring fields. Producing dairy products was another constant task and necessary to keep up with the quantity of milk. And those dairy products were also meant to sustain the families throughout winter, which meant there was always work to be done.

Historically, cows produced two-thirds of their annual milk during the summer farming period, and that milk was turned into food products to be stored and used throughout Norway's long, harsh winter. In the eighteen hundreds, there were close to 50,000 seters in operation throughout Norway. Most farms had one or more of these crucial mountain farms and at least part of the population spent the entire summer there caring for the animals. Today, there are about 1,000 mountain farms in operation, with around 60,000 goats and cows happily grazing and being milked throughout summer. Mountain farms are also home to non-milk producing cattle and goats, along with sheep, lamb, and pigs that graze on the land, cultivating the landscape and encouraging biological diversity.

Seter life is about more than just farming. It's also contributed to and helped shape the culinary culture in Norway. In fact, some of Norway's most iconic products and dishes, such as *rømmegrøt* ("sour cream porridge"), *brunost/geitost* ("brown cheese"), *prim* ("spreadable brown cheese"), *smør* ("butter"), and *mjølkekaker* ("milk cakes"), originate from the seter. Beyond their popularity, the quality of these foods is incomparable, with Norway boasting some of the best dairy products in the world. And it's no wonder, when the animals are feasting on wild berries and herbs, and living a life in which they are so well cared for and yet also free to roam.

Those working on seters are artisans and craftsman, skilled in milk production and cheesemaking. On the seter, small-scale processing is considered a treasured art form. The expertise and labor required to care for the animals and create so many traditional and unique products is not as easy to come by these days, but it's invaluable and important to sustaining this type of farming. Fortunately, there are those who continue to maintain this type of farming and lifestyle across Norway. It's still possible to visit a seter to experience, firsthand, the connection between nature, the animals, and the food. It's almost guaranteed that a warm bowl of rømmegrøt and a glass of homemade fruit juice will be waiting for you.

Homemade Butter

HJEMMELAGET SMØR

Butter has always played an important role in Norway. With little access to plant-derived fats, butter became essential for cooking, as well as an important means for the exchange of goods and the payment of taxes in Norwegian society.

Traditionally, butter produced at the seter was made with cream that sat for a couple days until it soured. It was then placed in a tall wooden kettle and churned until it separated, before being washed in the best water available from a nearby stream and finally strained of any remaining liquid.

The most luscious butter, which was called *fjellsmør/setersmør* ("mountain/seter butter"), had a bright yellow color and a fresh, creamy taste. It was always eaten right away. Butter meant to last through winter had to be heavily salted to avoid spoilage. This was the butter used in everyday cooking. Throughout winter, additional butter was made with little or no salt and used for baking.

Here, I've included two butter recipes, a seter butter made with sour cream and one made with heavy cream. The seter butter will be brighter yellow, but both are delicious.

each recipe makes about 14 ounces (400 g)

FOR THE SETER BUTTER
4¼ cups (1 l) whole milk sour cream
¼ teaspoon salt or more as needed

FOR THE REGULAR BUTTER
4¼ cups (1 l) heavy cream
¼ teaspoon salt or more as needed

Place the sour cream or heavy cream in the bowl of a stand mixer, whisk on low, gradually increasing the speed to medium-high. Continue whisking for 5 minutes or until the liquid separates from the mixture and a solid mass of butter forms. The liquid is buttermilk and should be refrigerated and reserved for baking.

Gather the butter solids and squeeze them between your hands, or press them through a mesh strainer or a piece of cheesecloth to remove any excess buttermilk. Run cold water over the butter and continue squeezing until all or most of the buttermilk is removed. If traces of buttermilk remain, the butter won't last as long.

Fold in the salt, adding more if desired, and refrigerate. The butter can be stored in parchment paper or an airtight container for up to 2 weeks, depending on how much buttermilk was extracted.

Brown Cheese

BRUNOST

One of Norway's most famous and beloved cheeses is sweet and nutty with a hint of caramel. The credit belongs to Anne Hov from Gudbrandsdalen, who, in 1863, experimented by adding cream to leftover whey and boiling it down to create a firm, cheese-like product. She later added goat's milk to give it a more distinctive taste and it became one of Norway's most iconic cheeses.

Typically, *brunost* is divided into those made of cow's milk (*fløtemysost*) and those made with the addition of goat's milk. For a milder flavor, I've used only cow's milk in this recipe. Brunost is often served thinly sliced on top of bread, waffles, and *svele* (griddle cakes). It's also added to some stews for flavor. • *makes about 10 ounces (280 g)*

12¾ cups (3 l) whole milk

4¼ cups (1 l) buttermilk

½ cup (120 ml) heavy cream

Line a colander with cheesecloth and set it over a large bowl.

In a large, heavy pot, heat the milk and buttermilk over medium-high heat, stirring often, until the curds and whey begin to separate. Using a slotted spoon, transfer the curds to the cheesecloth-lined colander. Remove from the heat.

Gather up the cheesecloth and squeeze any excess whey into the colander set over the large bowl. Return the excess whey to the pot. Save the curds; they make a delicious farm cheese.

Pour the whey through a mesh strainer into a second large, heavy pot and bring to a gentle simmer. If you find any curds, remove them with a strainer. Keep the whey at a constant simmer and cook, stirring occasionally, for 3½ to 4 hours or until thick. You might hear the whey "pop" once in a while. Using a wooden spoon, stir in the heavy cream. At this stage, the whey is what's called *prim*, a spreadable brown cheese. Cook for about 10 more minutes or until the cheese resembles a thick caramel sauce. Be careful not to cook all the moisture out; otherwise, it can be crumbly when cooled. Test by dropping a small amount on a plate and waiting a few minutes; if it firms up like a soft caramel when touched, it's ready. Stir a few more times to avoid graininess then remove from the heat.

Place the brown cheese in a prepared mold, such as a buttered ramekin or butter dish and let set. When ready, you may need a knife to remove the cheese from the mold. Wrap in a double layer of plastic wrap or place in an airtight container to prevent the cheese from drying out and refrigerate up to 4 weeks.

Sour Cream Porridge

RØMMEGRØT

The best *rømmegrøt* is always served at the seter and made with sour cream that's cooked down to a thick, creamy porridge. Nowadays rømmegrøt is enjoyed all year, but traditionally it was reserved for *Sankthans, Olsok,* and *Barsok,* the high holidays of summer. This was possibly because the best milk was produced in summer and the warm weather helped curdle the milk, making it a convenient dish to serve large groups.

My favorite rømmegrøt comes from the nearby Slettastølen seter run by my friend Sonja and her family. Sonja makes sour cream using raw milk from dairy cows that graze on the mountain pastures all summer long, which enriches their milk with an incomparable taste. She'll be the first to tell you that the key to proper rømmegrøt is using sour cream with a high percentage of fat, which in Norway means around 35 percent. Making rømmegrøt with lighter sour cream simply won't work. If you can't access proper sour cream, make your own with the recipe included here, but be sure to start a day ahead. This porridge topped with cinnamon and sugar can be served with cured meats. • *serves 4 to 6*

FOR THE HOMEMADE SOUR CREAM

2 cups (480 ml) heavy cream

½ cup (120 ml) buttermilk

FOR THE SOUR CREAM PORRIDGE

2 cups plus 1 tablespoon (500 ml) whole milk sour cream with 35% fat content

¾ cup plus 1 tablespoon (100 g) all-purpose flour, sifted

2 cups plus 1 tablespoon (500 ml) whole milk

Pinch of salt

Cinnamon and sugar, for serving

For the sour cream, combine the heavy cream and buttermilk in a clean glass jar with a lid. Seal the jar and let stand at room temperature for 24 hours then refrigerate until ready to use; the sour cream will thicken as it chills.

For the porridge, in a large, heavy saucepan, bring the sour cream to a gentle simmer. Continue simmering, stirring continuously, for about 10 minutes. Add about half the flour and stir vigorously until well blended. Stop stirring and return the mixture to a gentle simmer. Continue simmering for about 5 minutes or until the fat from the sour cream comes to the surface. With a spoon, remove as much fat as possible, reserving it to be served with the porridge. Add the remaining flour, stirring vigorously, and cook for 2 minutes longer to incorporate. Slowly add the milk, stirring to avoid lumps, and cook for 5 minutes or until smooth and creamy. Add the salt and combine.

Divide the porridge among bowls, top with cinnamon, sugar, and the reserved fat, and serve immediately.

Rice Porridge

RISENGRYNSGRØT

When rice porridge was first introduced to Norway in the thirteen hundreds, it was reserved for the wealthy and elite. It became customary to serve rice porridge on Christmas Eve, as a symbol of status, though it was typically eaten on Saturdays as well. In the eighteen hundreds, rice porridge spread to the working classes, who also prepared it on Saturdays and Christmas Eve.

Norwegians still serve rice porridge for Christmas Eve lunch and it's traditional to hide an almond in one of the bowls. Whoever finds the almond receives a prize, usually a small pig made of marzipan. As for non-holiday porridge, it's now enjoyed any day of the week, not just Saturday.

While rice porridge seems simple, it is memorable and comforting, like a soul-satisfying bowl of goodness. Slow cooking makes for incredibly creamy porridge, while adding cinnamon, sugar, and butter on top makes it completely irresistible. There's a reason this dish has been a steady favorite for so long. • *serves 4*

5½ cups (1.3 l) whole milk

½ vanilla bean, split and scraped

¾ cup plus 2 tablespoons (180 g) Arborio rice or medium-grain white rice

Lightly salted butter, cinnamon, and sugar, for serving

In a medium, heavy saucepan, combine the milk with the vanilla bean and seeds and place over medium heat. When the milk is warm to the touch, remove from the heat.

Place the rice in a separate medium, heavy saucepan over medium-high heat. Add about 1 cup (240 ml) of the warm milk and bring to a gentle simmer. Stirring frequently, continue simmering until most of the milk is absorbed by the rice. Repeat this process, adding milk, 1 cup (240 ml) at a time, and maintaining a gentle simmer until all the milk is added and the rice is creamy and thick but not too thick. Discard the vanilla bean.

Divide the porridge among bowls, top with butter, cinnamon, and sugar, and serve immediately.

Rhubarb and Juniper Berry Pie with a Sour Cream Crust

RABARBRAPAI MED EINERBÆR

———————

While pie is not a typical seter dish, it encompasses the warmth and coziness—a feeling known as *kos* or *hygge* in Norway—you feel at the farm in summer. I particularly love this combination of rhubarb and juniper berries, baked into a cocoon of sour cream pastry, because it draws you into life on the seter. You can almost see juniper shrubs in the background, rhubarb stalks in the garden, and fresh cream starting to sour in large milk cans.

This is a flavorful and aromatic pie and it's incredibly easy to work with the sour cream crust. Depending on the rhubarb used, the filling can be runny—stalks from the garden tend to release less liquid than larger ones from the store. For less runniness, thicken the filling with 5 tablespoons of instant tapioca instead of flour. • *serves 6 to 8*

FOR THE SOUR CREAM CRUST

2¼ cups (270 g) all-purpose flour, sifted

1 tablespoon granulated sugar, plus more for finishing

½ teaspoon salt

1 cup (224 g) cold, unsalted butter, cut into small pieces

½ cup (120 ml) sour cream

1 large egg, at room temperature and whisked with 1 teaspoon water

FOR THE RHUBARB FILLING

1¼ cups (250 g) granulated sugar

½ cup plus 2 tablespoons (80 g) all-purpose flour, sifted

1 teaspoon dried juniper berries

½ teaspoon cinnamon

½ teaspoon salt

27 ounces (755 g) rhubarb, cut into ½-inch (1.25 cm) pieces (about 6 cups total)

1 tablespoon freshly squeezed lemon juice

For the crust, combine the flour, sugar, and salt in a large bowl. Add the butter and use a pastry cutter or the tips of your fingers to quickly cut it into the flour mixture until it resembles bread-crumbs. Add the sour cream and blend together with a fork until a dough forms. Form the dough into 2 thick discs, wrap in plastic wrap, and refrigerate for at least 1 hour.

Remove the dough from the refrigerator and let stand for a few minutes at room temperature. On a lightly floured surface, use a rolling pin to roll out both discs into rounds large enough to fill a pie dish with about 1 inch (2.5 cm) overhang on all sides. Fit 1 round of dough into the pie dish, trimming any excess. Cut the second round into ¾-inch (2 cm) strips and refrigerate until ready to use.

Place a rimmed baking sheet in the center of the oven and preheat the oven to 425°F (220°C).

For the rhubarb filling, in a food processor, combine the sugar, flour, juniper berries, cinnamon, and salt and pulse until well blended. Strain the mixture through a mesh strainer set over a small bowl; discard any large pieces of juniper.

In a large bowl, combine the rhubarb and lemon juice. Add the sugar mixture and stir to combine. Pour into the prepared crust. Arrange the reserved strips of dough in an overlapping lattice pattern on top of the filling, pressing firmly on the edges to seal. Brush the dough with the egg and water mixture and sprinkle with sugar.

Place the pie on the rimmed baking sheet and bake for 15 minutes. Lower the oven temperature to 375°F (190°C) and bake for 35 minutes or until the crust is golden brown. Cool completely before serving.

No-Cook, Stirred Strawberry Jam

RØRTE JORDBÆR

On the seter table, you'll always find an array of fresh jams highlighting berries and other summer fruit. While some fruit is cooked down and canned to last through summer and into winter, the rest is made in the simplest and most satisfying way. Regardless of how they're prepared, all jams are served alongside the breads, cakes, cheeses, and sour cream that are also typical of the seter table.

This is one of the easiest "jam" recipes around. No cooking, no canning, and no preservatives are required, and because it's made with raw berries, this jam retains an incredibly fresh flavor. It won't keep as well as preserved jams, but once everyone starts digging in, it will disappear quickly anyway. Feel free to add more sugar to your liking, and depending upon the sweetness of the berries. · *makes 2 cups (500 ml)*

1 pound (450 g) fresh strawberries, hulled	¼ cup plus 2 tablespoons (75 g) granulated sugar

There are two main methods for making stirred jam. The first is to purée a third of the berries with the sugar then cut the remaining berries into small pieces and stir them into the purée.

The second method is to simply place the berries and sugar in a bowl and crush them with a fork until you reach the desired consistency.

Either jam can be stored in an airtight container in the refrigerator for up to 5 days.

Milk Cakes

MJØLKEKAKER

————————

On my second visit to Sonja's seter, she taught me how to make milk cakes, or what she refers to, in the local dialect, as *mjølkekaku*. These thin cakes are both airy and dense. They're also slightly addictive, so before you know it, you've eaten more than your fair share. Milk cakes are typical seter food; they're exactly the kind of treat you might expect to be served alongside your coffee. Sonja, of course, spared no expense, and served the cakes with all the trimmings, including homemade jams, spreadable cheeses, sour cream, and butter. She is, after all, a personification of Norwegian hospitality.

According to Sonja, milk cakes were traditionally made with only barley flour, but white flour was later added to make them more refined and luxurious. You'll notice there are no eggs in this recipe and that's because there were no hens at Sonja's family seter, so they made their cakes without. You can enjoy milk cakes on their own or with a topping of your choice.

makes about 30 cakes

4¼ cups (1 l) milk

1 cup plus ½ tablespoon (125 g) barley flour

2 cups plus 1 tablespoon (250 g) all-purpose flour, sifted

1 teaspoon baking soda

½ teaspoon salt

⅓ cup plus 1 tablespoon (100 ml) heavy cream

Lightly salted butter, for frying

In a large bowl, whisk together the milk, barley flour, all-purpose flour, baking soda, and salt. Add the heavy cream and whisk until the batter is lump free. Let stand for 30 minutes.

In a large griddle or heavy frying pan, heat a little butter over medium-high heat. Using a ladle, pour a little batter onto the hot griddle then use the bottom of the ladle to spread the batter in a circular motion until it's about 8 inches (20 cm) in diameter—the cakes will have a circular pattern imprinted on them. Cook for about 1 minute or until the cake is golden brown on the bottom then flip and cook 1 minute or until the other side is golden brown. If the cakes stick, use a spatula to occasionally loosen them from the griddle as they cook. Repeat with the remaining batter, adding more butter to the griddle as needed.

Serve the milk cakes warm with any combination of butter, sugar, spreadable brown cheese (*prim*), sour cream, and jams.

Light and Fluffy Cheesecake

OSTEKAKE

In the seventeen hundreds, cheesecakes reflected the tastes of the times and what was available. They were typically made with fresh cheese curds, cream, eggs, butter, sugar, and currants, and seasoned with cloves, nutmeg, and rosewater. Today, you'll find cheesecakes similar to New York-style versions, with cream cheese being the star ingredient. One big difference, however, is that the Norwegian variety often uses flavored gelatins in and on top of the cake.

My mother-in-law, Kari, makes one of the best cheesecakes around. It's her most requested dessert and I'm incredibly pleased that she's happy for me to share her recipe. It's a light variation on what can be quite a heavy dessert and it requires no baking. Her filling has a subtle touch of lemon, while the base has a buttery, sweet, and salty taste that literally melts in your mouth.

Kari uses lemon-flavored gelatin powder, but only folded into the batter, so there's no wiggly layer of gelatin on top. This creates a delicate balance of velvety texture and buoyancy, without taking away from the simplicity of this delightful dessert. • *serves 8 to 10*

½ pound (225 g) digestive biscuits, roughly crushed

½ cup (112 g) lightly salted butter, melted

1 cup plus 2 teaspoons (250 ml) water

4½ ounces (125 g) lemon-flavored gelatin powder

½ pound (225 g) cream cheese

1¼ cups (300 ml) light sour cream

1 cup (120 g) confectioners' sugar

1¼ cups (300 ml) heavy cream

Seasonal fruit, to garnish (optional)

Butter a 9-inch (23 cm) springform pan then line the pan with parchment paper and butter the paper.

In a large bowl, stir together the crushed biscuits and melted butter. Press the biscuit mixture into the bottom of the prepared pan and refrigerate until ready to use.

In a small saucepan, bring the water to a boil. Add the gelatin and stir until completely dissolved. Pour into a medium, heat-safe bowl and let cool completely. Add the cream cheese and stir to fully combine.

In a second large bowl, whisk together the sour cream and confectioners' sugar. Add the cream cheese-gelatin mixture and whisk to combine.

In a second medium bowl, whisk the heavy cream until stiff peaks form then add to the batter and gently fold to combine.

Pour the batter over the biscuit crust, smooth the top, and refrigerate for at least 2 hours or until set.

Serve plain or topped with seasonal fruit.

Caramel Pudding

KARAMELLPUDDING

———

This is one of the most popular milk-based desserts in Norway. I have fond memories of my Norwegian family serving it during the holidays, but it can be enjoyed throughout the year. This recipe was passed down from a friend of the family and always receives rave reviews. • *serves 8*

FOR THE CARAMEL

¾ cup plus 1 tablespoon (165 g) granulated sugar

FOR THE PUDDING

2½ cups (600 ml) whole milk

1¼ cups (300 ml) heavy cream

⅓ cup (65 g) granulated sugar

1 vanilla bean, split and scraped

8 large eggs, at room temperature

Preheat the oven to 250°F (120°C).

For the caramel, in a large, heavy pot, heat the sugar over medium-high heat, stirring constantly with a wooden spoon, until the sugar breaks down and is a golden color. Immediately pour into a loaf pan no smaller than 8½ x 4½ x 2½ inches (21 x 11 x 6 cm) and set aside to harden.

For the pudding, in a medium, heavy saucepan, combine the milk, heavy cream, sugar, and the vanilla bean and seeds and heat over medium heat, stirring occasionally, until the sugar has dissolved and the mixture is warm to the touch. Remove from the heat.

In a large bowl, whisk the eggs just to combine, being careful not to add too much air. Remove the vanilla bean from the milk mixture and slowly pour into the eggs, whisking constantly for a smooth consistency. Gently pour the mixture through a mesh strainer and into the caramel-lined loaf pan.

Set the loaf pan in a deep roasting pan then add enough boiling water to the roasting pan to go one third up the side of the loaf pan. Bake for 2 hours or until the pudding is set. To test, dip the back of a spoon in the hot water then press gently on top of the pudding. If it bounces back and is stiff, it's ready. Carefully remove the loaf pan from the roasting pan and let cool completely. Refrigerate the pudding for at least 4 hours and preferably overnight to give the pudding time to absorb the caramel sauce.

Run a blunt knife around the edges of the pudding to loosen it then set a large serving platter on top and carefully flip it over. Lift the loaf pan from the pudding; the caramel sauce should pour onto the platter. Serve with whipped cream and fruit.

Layered Cream Cake with Fresh Berries

BLØTKAKE

Bløtkake is the quintessential Norwegian party cake. With its light and fluffy sponge and delightfully sweet and tangy berries, it is, without a doubt, one of the most beloved cakes. It always makes an appearance when there's something to celebrate, but it's so good, it can—and should—be served any day of the week.

There are slight variations across recipes, but most versions feature whipped cream, jam, and sometimes custard, sandwiched between layers of vanilla sponge. Bløtkake is topped with more whipped cream and fruit, and can be covered in a blanket of marzipan. It tends to taste better a day or two after you make it, because the flavors have a chance to come together. · *serves 8 to 10*

5 large eggs, at room temperature

¾ cup plus 2 tablespoons (175 g) granulated sugar

1½ cups (180 g) all-purpose flour, sifted

1 teaspoon baking powder

2½ cups (600 ml) heavy cream

2½ tablespoons confectioners' sugar

½ cup (120 ml) milk or juice, such as orange or apple

Strawberry jam, for assembling

Mixed berries, for decorating

Preheat the oven to 325°F (165°C).

Cut a round piece of parchment paper so it fits perfectly in the bottom of a 9-inch (23 cm) springform pan. Butter the pan then add the parchment and butter the parchment.

In a stand mixer, whisk the eggs and granulated sugar on medium-high for 6 to 8 minutes or until stiff and light in color. Sift the flour and baking powder over the batter and use a rubber spatula to gently fold until just combined. Pour into the prepared pan and set on a baking sheet. Bake in the middle of the oven for 35 to 40 minutes or until golden brown. Let cool completely.

In a large bowl, whip the heavy cream and confectioners' sugar until stiff peaks form.

To assemble, cut the cake horizontally into 3 even layers. Place the bottom layer, cut-side up, on a serving plate or platter. Spoon half of the milk or juice over the bottom layer then top with a layer of strawberry jam, followed by a generous amount of whipped cream, spreading it to the edges of the cake. Arrange the second layer of cake on top and repeat the process of adding milk or juice, jam, and whipped cream, reserving enough whipped cream to cover the cake. Top with the final cake layer then cover the top and sides of the cake with the remaining whipped cream. The cake can be served immediately or, to allow the cake to soften and soak up more flavor, made and stored in the refrigerator up to 1 day in advance. Decorate the top with berries and serve.

Rommegrøt Ice Cream

RØMMEGRØT-ISKREM

The inspiration for this recipe came from my first ice cream experience in Norway. I remember waiting in line for a *softis* (soft-serve ice cream) one sunny summer day. One after another, people walked away with towering cones covered in a dark powder. It was my first introduction to softis dipped in chocolate powder, which perfectly coats the vanilla soft serve, and provides just the right amount of chocolate flavor.

Reminiscing about this experience gave me the idea to take rommegrøt, the classic sour cream porridge that's practically coated with cinnamon and sugar, and put it in a cone. My ice cream version maintains the sweet, tangy flavors without being so heavy and is rather refreshing on hot days. It starts with a simple sour cream–base, and is topped with a generous dusting of cinnamon sugar for a cooled-down take on the traditional dish. And since rømmegrøt is often served with cured meats, tossing a couple pieces of fried Norwegian *fenalår* on top adds a bit of fun texture and flavor. • *makes about 2 pints (1 l)*

1¼ cups (300 g) whole milk sour cream
1¼ cups (300 ml) heavy cream
¾ cup (150 g) granulated sugar

Cinnamon and sugar, for topping
Cured meats like fenalår (see page 154), for topping (optional)

In a medium bowl, whisk together the sour cream, heavy cream, and sugar. Refrigerate until cold. Pour the mixture into an ice cream machine and follow the manufacturer's instructions to process. Alternatively, pour the mixture into an airtight plastic container and freeze at least 3 to 4 hours or until hardened.

When ready to serve, in a small bowl, mix together the sugar and cinnamon. I recommend a 4 to 1 ratio—4 tablespoons sugar to 1 tablespoon cinnamon, for example—and generously sprinkle over the ice cream. Serve immediately.

Innhøstingen

THE HARVEST

The harvest is a joyous time, when the fields overflow

with excess and nature's bounty can be collected and relished. It's a culmination and celebration of the year's hard work, as well as a time to gather crops and other edible ingredients to be preserved for the coming months.

Norway has a long farming tradition. In the nineteenth century, almost 90 percent of the population lived outside cities and most were involved in agriculture or fishing. Barley and oats were the main grain crops, but in the warmer climates of eastern Norway, and in Trøndelag, in the center of the country, wheat was also grown. Cultivating potatoes, along with other root vegetables, also became quite popular.

Nowadays, crop varieties can vary slightly or drastically between regions and from the northern part of the country to the southern part, as well as from inland to the coast. This is because growing certain crops depends on the geography and climate of the area and those characteristics often differ throughout Norway.

If you head along the fjords in western Norway, you can taste the most incredible apples, cherries, pears, raspberries, and plums. The Hardanger region is responsible for half the national fruit production—apples are the most famous crop—while Sogn og Fjordane has the largest raspberry production in the country.

The eastern region, Østlandet, has the most ideal climate for agriculture in all of Norway. Most of the country's vegetables, including potatoes, rutabaga, celeriac, parsnips, Jerusalem artichokes, turnips, cabbage, cauliflower, and broccoli, along with berries and other fruit, are grown in this region's valleys.

In southern Norway, mostly vegetables are grown, with potatoes and some fruit along the coast. Moving toward the middle of the country, the area of Trøndelag cultivates potatoes and vegetables, plus berries and other fruit, as you move toward the coast. Northern Norway has only a modest amount of farmland yet it possesses prime conditions for growing quality food, thanks to the midnight sun—when the sun remains visible for most of the day during the summer months—and very few threats to the crops.

Aside from cultivated crops, Norway has always relied heavily on sheep and cattle for both meat and milk production. In the autumn, around early September, it's tradition to return the animals from the seter ("summer mountain farm") to the main farm, in a process known as *sausanking* or "sheep foraging." This is a special time when days are carefully planned and established methods are used to move animals across the terrain, guided by both people and shepherd dogs. Days are set aside, bags are packed, and groups of people take on this task together, moving and guiding the sheep, bundling in sleeping bags in one-room cabins, and sharing communal meals. If the weather is favorable, the experience is said to be one of the most beautiful and remarkable excursions one can have in nature.

Once the sheep return to the main farm, the inevitable must occur. Those that have grown big and strong go straight to the slaughterhouse, while others spend a few more weeks at the farm to achieve the right weight. This is the time of year when lamb is the showcase of many meals. Since the animals grazed on grass and wild herbs all summer long, their meat takes on exceptional flavor. *Fårikål*, a lamb and cabbage stew, is, arguably, the best way to feature such a wonderful autumn bounty; it's also Norway's national dish.

In this chapter, you'll find a variety of recipes that celebrate the harvest and are ideal for høst, or "autumn." Harvesting takes place throughout the year, of course, and includes what comes from the waters, but here, I focus primarily on autumn's cultivated crops—although some are gathered throughout the summer season as well—and meat production.

Rustic Savory Pear Tart

PÆRETERTE

Norwegians are incredibly giving people who are usually more than happy to share what they have. I find this to be particularly true during harvest season, when neighbors bring fresh produce around or ask you to come and take what you want from their fields.

As we don't have pear trees ourselves, when autumn arrives, I always look forward to receiving a basketful from friends. This tart is one of my favorite dishes to make. It not only celebrates the harvest season, but it also highlights locally made products. While the combination of pears, walnuts, blue cheese, and honey is nothing new, it makes for a truly warming treat when paired with homemade whole-wheat puff pastry. · *serves 15*

FOR THE WHOLE-WHEAT PUFF PASTRY

1 cup (120 g) coarse whole-wheat flour

1 cup (120 g) all-purpose flour, sifted

1 teaspoon salt

½ cup (120 ml) ice water

1 cup (224 g) lightly salted butter, cold and cut into 4 pieces

FOR THE TART

8 small or 4 large pears, halved lengthwise, cored, and thinly sliced

4½ ounces (125 g) crumbled blue cheese

¾ cup (75 g) walnuts, coarsely chopped

Honey, for drizzling

For the whole-wheat puff pastry, in a medium bowl, whisk the whole-wheat and all-purpose flours with the salt. Transfer the mixture to a clean surface and make a well in the center. Add a little of the ice water to the well and, using your hands or a fork, gently toss with the flour. Continue adding the rest of the water until the dough comes together, adding more water as needed. Press the dough into a square, wrap in plastic wrap, and refrigerate at least 30 minutes.

Arrange the butter pieces side by side and place between 2 sheets of parchment paper. Using a rolling pin, pound the butter gently to flatten and soften it. Fold the butter on to itself and continue pounding until quite pliable. Shape the butter into a 5 x 5-inch (13 x 13 cm) square, wrap in plastic wrap, and refrigerate at least 30 minutes.

On a lightly floured surface, roll out the dough into a square large enough for the butter to fit in the center with a 3-inch (7.5 cm) border. Wrap the dough around the butter overlapping it and pinching the edges to seal. Turn the dough over, so the folded side sits directly on the lightly floured surface. Flour the rolling pin and roll out the dough into a long rectangle. Fold the top ⅓ of the rectangle down to the center, then fold the bottom ⅓ up and over that, like you would fold a letter. Rotate the dough a quarter turn and roll out into another long rectangle. Fold like a letter as before then wrap in plastic wrap and refrigerate for 30 minutes. This is 2 turns.

Repeat the rolling out, folding, and chilling process 2 more times for a total of 6 turns. If you notice any butter coming through the dough, pat it with a little flour. Wrap in plastic wrap and refrigerate at least 30 minutes.

Preheat the oven to 400°F (200°C). Line a baking sheet with parchment paper.

On a lightly floured surface, roll out the dough into a rectangle large enough to fill a baking sheet and about ¼-inch (½ cm) thick. Transfer the dough to the parchment-lined baking sheet. Use a fork to poke holes throughout, avoiding the edges, to prevent the dough from bubbling up.

Arrange the pear slices over the entire surface of the dough, leaving a 1-inch (2.5 cm) border and overlapping the pears slightly so they're very close together. Sprinkle the blue cheese and walnuts over the pears, generously drizzle with honey, and bake for 30 minutes or until golden brown and bubbling. Let cool slightly.

Cut the tart into squares, drizzle with more honey, if desired, and serve warm.

Creamy Jerusalem Artichoke Soup

KREMET JORDSKOKKSUPPE

The earliest written record of the Jerusalem artichoke in Norway is a description from a 1694 horticultural book. It was a fairly prevalent vegetable and featured prominently in the cuisine. However, in the eighteen hundreds, the potato began to take hold and the Jerusalem artichoke diminished in popularity and became less common. Even to this day, the Jerusalem artichoke is hard to come by and not particularly well known. The good news is that it's making a comeback.

This recipe comes from my dear friend Maj-Lis, who is incredibly passionate when it comes to maintaining tradition in her cooking, but who also likes to incorporate influences from other cultures. Rich and creamy, it's a perfect autumn soup, and incredibly simple to make. There's a sweetness to this dish that's complemented by a topping of dried mushrooms or fried pieces of Jerusalem artichoke. It's best served in smaller quantities, as an appetizer or accompaniment to another dish. • *serves 6 to 8*

4¼ cups (1 liter) vegetable or chicken stock

2½ cups (600 ml) whole milk

1⅔ cups (400 ml) heavy cream

½ pound (225 g) Jerusalem artichokes, peeled and cut into cubes

⅓ cup plus 2 tablespoons (100 g) lightly salted butter, cut into small pieces

Salt and pepper

Dried mushrooms or fried slices of Jerusalem artichoke, for garnish

In a large, heavy pot, combine the stock, milk, and heavy cream and bring to a gentle simmer. Add the Jerusalem artichokes and simmer for about 20 to 30 minutes or until tender. Using a slotted spoon, transfer the Jerusalem artichokes to a blender or food processor. Add the butter and a little soup to the blender and purée until smooth, being careful of the heat. Return to the pot and stir until heated through and combined.

To serve, fry some dried mushrooms in a little oil or simply sprinkle the dried mushrooms on top of the soup, as Maj-Lis does. Alternatively, fry some thin slices of Jerusalem artichoke in a little oil and use those as garnish.

Cauliflower Soup Topped with Fried Fennel

BLOMKÅLSUPPE MED FENNIKEL

This is a classic, everyday Norwegian soup. I like that it isn't too fancy and that it's all about the cauliflower. It's also simple to make, especially since the stock used is just the water the cauliflower is boiled in. I enjoy it topped with sautéed fennel and a drizzle of cream. • *serves 4*

2 pounds (900 g) cauliflower, roughly chopped

½ cup (120 ml) heavy cream, plus more for serving

Salt and white pepper

1 large fennel bulb with fronds

1 tablespoon lightly salted butter

1 tablespoon mild-flavored oil, plus more for serving

In a large, heavy pot, combine the cauliflower with enough cold salted water to cover and bring to a boil. Continue boiling until the cauliflower can be easily pierced with a knife. Drain the cauliflower, reserving the cooking water.

In a food processor or blender, purée the cauliflower, adding some of the reserved cooking water as needed to make it smooth—you'll need about half of the water. Return the soup to the pot and stir in the heavy cream. Season to taste with salt and white pepper. Keep warm.

Cut off and discard the stalks from fennel bulbs, reserving the fronds for garnish. Slice the fennel bulb lengthwise into thin strips. In a large sauté pan, heat the butter and oil over medium-high heat. Add the fennel and sauté until starting to brown and caramelize, with some crispy pieces.

Divide the soup among bowls and top with the sautéed fennel. Drizzle with a little heavy cream or oil, garnish with the fennel fronds, and serve.

Sweet and Sour Braised Red Cabbage

RØDKÅL

While cabbage has been an integral part of the Norwegian kitchen for centuries, this particular recipe was most likely borrowed from Denmark. The original Danish dish was sour and made with green cabbage until a period of nationalism in the eighteen hundreds inspired the Danes to switch to red cabbage to reflect the color of their flag. After sugar became available, it evolved into the sweet and sour dish it is today.

These days, recipes for *rødkål* contain a variety of ingredients from apples, raisins, prunes, and fruit juice to brown sugar, red wine, pork fat, and spices. It's the kind of dish that you taste and adjust to your liking as you go along. It's also one that doesn't require a lot of attention, so you can take care of other things while it simmers away on the stove.

Rødkål is typically reserved for Christmas Eve, and most often paired with *ribbe* (pork belly ribs) and potatoes. I also happen to think it's a great side dish to make when cabbage is freshly harvested in autumn. If you don't have blackcurrant cordial, use red wine instead and add a little more honey. · *serves 6*

2¼ pounds (1 kg) red cabbage

2 tablespoons lightly salted butter

⅓ cup plus 1 tablespoon (100 ml) black currant cordial

⅓ cup plus 1 tablespoon (100 ml) apple juice

3 tablespoons plus 1 teaspoon (50 ml) apple cider vinegar

2 tablespoons honey

1 teaspoon whole cloves

1 teaspoon salt

Remove the outer leaves of the cabbage, cut in half, and remove the core. Finely chop.

In a large, heavy pot, melt the butter over medium-high heat. Add the cabbage and stir to coat in the butter. Add the black currant cordial, apple juice, apple cider vinegar, honey, cloves, and salt and bring to a gentle boil. Lower the heat, cover, and gently simmer, stirring occasionally, for 2 to 2½ hours or until the cabbage is soft. When the cabbage is almost finished, taste and add more cordial, vinegar, or honey, as needed. Remove the lid, raise the heat, and bring to a boil, stirring frequently, for 2 to 3 minutes or until most of the liquid evaporates, leaving just a glaze on the cabbage. Set aside to cool.

Rødkål can be served right away, but it will deepen in flavor the longer it sits and is even better the next day. Store, covered, in the refrigerator for a couple days. This dish can be served warm or cold.

Lamb and Cabbage Stew

FÅRIKÅL

Fårikål is Norway's national dish, but the term *får-i-kål*, which means "lamb in cabbage," is of Danish origin and the dish itself existed outside of Norway before it became a national staple in the twentieth century. Despite its non-native origins, fårikål is beloved, perhaps because the ingredients so perfectly represent Norway's bounty. There's lamb from the mountains, potatoes just harvested from the fields, and fresh cabbage that grows all summer. Together, they form a little piece of Norway.

Fårikål's layers of cabbage and lamb are studded with whole black peppercorns. According to tradition, peppercorns aid digestion and should be eaten with the dish, but nowadays, many people simply brush them off before diving in. The flour helps thicken the stew a little as it cooks, but can be omitted for a gluten-free version. The cabbage contains a lot of water that will be released as it cooks, so resist any urges to add more water than the stated amount.

Enjoy this hearty stew with boiled potatoes, flatbread, and a glass of locally brewed beer—and earn extra points if you serve it on the last Thursday in September, which is fårikål's national day, known as *fårikålens festdag*. It will be a true Norwegian experience and you'll be the better for it. *serves 6 to 8*

4½ pounds (2 kg) good-quality lamb on the bone, such as neck, shoulder, or shank meat, cut into about 1¼-inch-thick (3 cm) pieces (ask your butcher to cut the pieces)

½ cup (60 g) all-purpose flour

1⅔ cups (400 ml) water

4½ pounds (2 kg) white cabbage, cored and cut into large wedges

5 teaspoons whole black peppercorns

4 teaspoons salt

Lightly salted butter, for serving (optional)

In a bowl, toss the lamb with the flour.

Pour the water into a large, heavy pot. Arrange a layer of the floured lamb on the bottom of the dish, followed by a layer of cabbage. Sprinkle with some of the peppercorns and some of the salt. Repeat this process until you've used all the ingredients and finish with a final layer of cabbage on top. Cover and bring to a boil. Lower the heat and gently cook for about 2½ hours or until the lamb is tender and falling off the bone.

Serve hot with boiled potatoes and a good dab of butter if desired.

Beer-Braised Lamb Shanks with Root Vegetables

ØLBRAISERTE LAMMESKANKER

———

As September arrives in Norway so does the annual herding that takes lambs from the mountain pastures to their respective farms. Those lambs that have grown big and strong will go straight to the slaughterhouse, but the rest will spend a few more weeks at the farm until they reach the ideal weight. Throughout this season, lamb is the highlight of many dishes and since the animals have grazed on grass and wild herbs all summer long, their meat has exceptional flavor. When it comes to cooking lamb shanks, I like to braise them in dark ale, along with root vegetables. The result is a rich and deeply flavored stew, with the meat falling off the bone. • *serves 4*

1 large fennel bulb with fronds

3 tablespoons mild-flavored oil

4 lamb shanks

3 tablespoons lightly salted butter

2 medium carrots, peeled and chopped

1 large onion, chopped

1 small rutabaga, peeled and chopped

1 medium parsnip, peeled and chopped

17 ounces (500 ml) dark ale

2 bay leaves

¼ cup (60 ml) apple cider vinegar

Salt and pepper

Fresh flat-leaf parsley, for garnish (optional)

Cut off and discard the stalks from the fennel bulb, reserving the fronds for garnish; chop the bulb.

In a large, heavy pot, heat the oil over medium-high heat. Working in batches as needed, add the lamb shanks and sear, turning, for 2 to 3 minutes or until brown on all sides. Remove from the pot and set aside; repeat with the remaining lamb shanks.

Add the butter to the lamb pot and melt over medium-high heat. Add the chopped fennel, carrots, onion, rutabaga, and parsnip and sauté for about 10 minutes or until starting to caramelize. Return the lamb shanks to the pot. Add the beer and bring to a boil. Add the bay leaves and apple cider vinegar and season to taste with salt and pepper. Lower the heat and gently simmer for 2½ hours or until the meat is falling off the bone. Transfer the lamb to a serving platter and cover with foil. Discard the bay leaves and bring the sauce to a boil. Continue boiling until reduced by a third or to the desired consistency.

Pour the sauce over the lamb and garnish with parsley or fennel fronds. Serve warm with mashed potatoes.

Norwegian Meatballs with Creamed Cabbage

KJØTTKAKER MED KÅLSTUING

––––––––

Meatballs are one of the most well-known Nordic dishes, though variations are found globally. Within the Nordic region, the recipes are quite similar, but can be made with different meats and spices. Norwegians, like their Nordic neighbors, hold meatballs in such high regard that *kjøttkaker* was a top contender for Norway's national dish.

Norwegian meatballs are traditionally served with brown gravy, boiled potatoes, lingonberry jam, and either a pea stew or creamed cabbage. It's a great dish to serve when the vegetables have just been harvested and the weather is beginning to cool. • *serves 6*

FOR THE MEATBALLS

1½ pounds (680 g) ground beef

1½ teaspoons salt

1 teaspoon white pepper

½ teaspoon ground nutmeg

½ teaspoon ground ginger

1 small red onion, finely chopped

3 tablespoons potato starch

1 large egg

1 cup (240 ml) milk

2 tablespoons mild-flavored oil

FOR THE BROWN SAUCE

6 tablespoons (80 g) lightly salted butter

½ cup plus 2 tablespoons (80 g) all-purpose flour

4¼ cups (1 l) beef stock

¼ teaspoon salt

White pepper

FOR THE CREAMED CABBAGE

1 tablespoon salt

7 cups (700 g) chopped cabbage, about 1 head cabbage

4 tablespoons (56g) lightly salted butter

½ cup (60 g) all-purpose flour

2 cups plus 1 tablespoon (500 ml) milk

Pinch of ground nutmeg

White pepper

For the meatballs, in a food processor, blend the ground beef with the salt, pepper, nutmeg, and ginger. With the processor running, add the red onion, followed by the potato starch, and lastly the egg and milk then pulse until smooth. Have a bowl of warm water nearby. Dip a large spoon in the water then use the spoon to scoop the meat and use your hands to form 16 large meatballs.

In a large, heavy skillet, heat the oil over medium-high heat. Working in batches, add the meatballs and cook, turning, for 5 minutes or until brown on all sides. Transfer to a plate and set aside.

For the brown sauce, in a large, heavy saucepan, melt the butter over medium heat. Whisk in the flour and cook, whisking frequently, for 6 to 8 minutes or until dark brown—be careful not to burn the flour. Slowly add the beef stock, whisking to combine, and salt. Add the meatballs and bring to a boil. Lower the heat and gently simmer for 15 minutes or until the meatballs are cooked through. Season to taste with salt and pepper.

While the meatballs are cooking, make the cabbage: Bring a large saucepan of water to a boil. Add the salt and cabbage and boil for 15 minutes or until the cabbage can be easily pierced with a knife. Drain the cabbage and set aside. In the same pan, melt the butter over medium-high heat. Whisk in the flour and cook, whisking frequently for 2 minutes. Add the milk and nutmeg and cook, whisking frequently, until thick. Fold in the cabbage and season to taste with salt and pepper.

Serve the meatballs and creamed cabbage with boiled potatoes, stewed green peas (or cooked fresh peas), and lingonberry jam.

Plum Jam and Almond Custard Sweet Buns

SNURRER MED PLOMMESYLTETØY OG MANDELKREM

Plums have been cultivated in Norway since the seventeen hundreds, which makes cooking plums a 300-year-old Norwegian tradition. We always seem to have more than enough plums on the farm and excess usually means one thing: jam. Here, I put the jam to good use in these sweet buns. I admit they're a little indulgent, but that tends to happen when autumn is at its height and winter is peeking its head around the corner. I like to mix custard with almond cream and use that as a filling for my buns, along with homemade plum jam. It's a messy process, but the outcome is well worth it. · *makes 12 large buns*

FOR THE BUN DOUGH

1 cup (240 ml) milk

½ cup plus 1 tablespoon (125 g) lightly salted butter

5 cups (600 g) all-purpose flour, sifted

½ cup plus 2 tablespoons (125 g) granulated sugar

2 ounces (50 g) fresh yeast or ⅔ ounce (17 g) active dry yeast

1 teaspoon ground cinnamon

1 large egg, at room temperature

FOR THE ALMOND CREAM

⅔ cup (110 g) ground almonds

½ cup plus 1 tablespoon (115 g) granulated sugar

½ cup (112 g) lightly salted butter

2 large eggs, at room temperature

2 tablespoons all-purpose flour, sifted

⅛ teaspoon salt

FOR THE CUSTARD

¼ cup (50 g) granulated sugar

2 large egg yolks

2 tablespoons cornstarch

1 cup (240 ml) whole milk

½ vanilla bean, split and scraped

1 cup (240 ml) plum jam or compote

For the dough, combine the milk and butter in a small saucepan over medium heat and heat until the butter is melted. Remove from the heat.

In a stand mixer fitted with the dough hook attachment, combine the flour, sugar, yeast, and cinnamon. Add the warm milk mixture and start kneading on medium-low to combine. Add the egg and continue kneading for about 8 minutes or until the dough is soft, smooth, and elastic. Resist the urge to add more flour. Cover with a tea towel and let rise in a warm spot for 1½ hours or until doubled in size.

For the almond cream, in a stand mixer fitted with the paddle attachment, beat together the ground almonds, sugar, butter, eggs, flour, and salt. Set aside.

For the custard, in a medium bowl, whisk together the sugar and egg yolks. Add the cornstarch and whisk until thick and pale yellow. In a medium, heavy saucepan, combine the milk with the vanilla bean and seeds and warm over medium heat until just beginning to simmer then immediately remove from the heat. Slowly add the milk to the egg yolk mixture, whisking constantly to avoid curdling the eggs. Pour the mixture back into the saucepan and place over

medium heat. Cook, stirring constantly, until thick. Let cool completely then gently combine with the almond cream. Refrigerate the almond custard for at least 15 minutes.

Preheat the oven to 425°F (220°C). Line two baking sheets with parchment paper.

On a well-floured surface, use a rolling pin to roll out the dough into a large rectangle that measures roughly 18 × 22 inches (45 × 56 cm), with the longer side directly in front of you. Spread about 1 cup (240 ml) of the almond custard over the entire surface of the dough, spreading it to the edges. Reserve the remaining almond custard for another use. Spread the plum jam in ½-inch (1.25 cm) thick vertical lines on top of the almond custard, evenly spacing the lines, so they are about 4 inches (10 cm) apart. If the jam is too thick, heat it in a saucepan so it's easier to spread. Gently roll the dough horizontally, from left to right to form a log. Using a sharp knife, cut the log into 12 pieces. Arrange the buns on the parchment-lined baking sheets and bake, 1 sheet at a time, for 10 to 12 minutes or until nicely browned. Set on a wire rack to cool completely before serving.

Veiled Peasant Girls

TILSLØRTE BONDEPIKER

———————

This old-fashioned dessert featuring layers of stewed apples, sweetened breadcrumbs, and whipped cream, was extremely popular before ice cream became common throughout Norway.

The name, *Tilslørte bondepiker* or "Veiled Peasant Girls," is somewhat of a mystery, though one legend suggests it came from the famous Norwegian poet, Ivar Aasen. As the story goes, Aasen fell in love with a peasant girl, who repeatedly turned down his affections. One day, she offered him a taste of her sweets and he was quite disappointed to learn she was referring to this dessert. In his frustration, Aasen named the dessert "veiled peasant girls." It's also possible the "veil" refers to the blanket of whipped cream on top.

Whatever the reasons behind the name, this dessert is quick to make and incredibly delicious. It's ideal for when fresh apples are available. Be sure to use firm, tart apples and leave the skins on for beautiful color. I recommend serving this dessert right away, while the crumbs are still crispy.
serves 4

FOR THE STEWED APPLES

8 small, tart apples, cored and diced (about 5 cups total)

½ cup (100 g) granulated sugar

⅓ cup plus 1 tablespoon (100 ml) water

1 tablespoon freshly squeezed lemon juice

FOR THE BREADCRUMBS

4 tablespoons (56 g) lightly salted butter

1½ cups (90 g) breadcrumbs

¼ cup (50 g) granulated sugar

3 teaspoons ground cinnamon

FOR THE WHIPPED CREAM

1¼ cups (300 ml) heavy cream

½ vanilla bean, split and scraped

Toasted hazelnuts or walnuts, for garnish (optional)

For the stewed apples, in a medium, heavy saucepan, combine the apples, sugar, water, and lemon juice over medium heat and bring to a gentle simmer. Continue simmering for 5 minutes or until the apples are soft. Remove from the heat then stir and mash the mixture slightly, leaving some chunkier pieces. Set aside to cool.

For the breadcrumbs, in a medium, heavy pan, melt the butter over medium-low heat. Add the breadcrumbs, sugar, and cinnamon and sauté, stirring constantly, for about 5 minutes or until golden brown. Set aside to cool.

For the whipped cream, in a large bowl, combine the heavy whipping cream and vanilla seeds and whip until stiff peaks form.

To assemble, on individual plates or in individual glasses, layer the stewed apples, breadcrumbs, and whipped cream at least 2 times, finishing with the whipped cream on top. Garnish with extra breadcrumbs and toasted hazelnuts or walnuts, if using. Serve immediately.

Apple Cake

EPLEKAKE

———————

Parts of Norway seamlessly transform into striking orchards in the autumn, with branches full of sweet yet tart and incredibly crisp apples. The history of apples in Norway and northern Europe stretches back at least as far as the Stone Age and findings from the Oseberg Viking ship, revealed fifty-four well-preserved wild apples.

One of Norway's most beloved apple desserts is *eplekake*, a simple and unassuming cake that's not overly sweet or too heavy. The sweetness of the sponge cake is complemented by the tanginess of the apples and you get just a hint of cinnamon and crunch from the brown sugar–almond topping. · *serves 8 to 10*

2 cups (240 g) all-purpose flour, sifted

1½ teaspoons baking powder

1¼ cups (250 g) granulated sugar

¾ cup (150 g) lightly salted butter, at room temperature, plus more for topping

3 large eggs, at room temperature

½ cup (120 ml) milk

3 to 4 tart apples, peeled, cored and thinly sliced

⅓ cup (33 g) sliced almonds

2 tablespoons dark brown sugar

1 tablespoon ground cinnamon

Whipped cream or ice cream, for serving

Preheat the oven to 350°F (180°C). Butter an 8-inch (20 cm) springform pan.

In a medium bowl, whisk together the flour and baking powder.

In the bowl of a stand mixer fitted with the paddle attachment, beat the sugar and butter until light and fluffy. Add the eggs, 1 at a time, incorporating each egg before adding the next one, and beat for 2 to 3 minutes or until light and creamy. Add the flour mixture and blend. Slowly add the milk and beat just until well blended. Pour the batter into the prepared pan. Place the apple slices on top of the batter, arranging them in tightly overlapping concentric circles and gently pressing them into the batter. Sprinkle with the almonds, brown sugar, and cinnamon. Arrange a couple dabs of butter on top and bake for about 1 hour or until a toothpick inserted in the center comes out clean and the top of the cake is golden brown with a few dark spots from the cinnamon. Cool slightly in the pan before serving with whipped cream or ice cream.

Carrot Sheet Cake

GULROTKAKE

Carrot cake is one of the more popular cakes in Norway. In the Middle Ages, before the introduction of sugar, cakes often featured carrots because of their natural sweetness. Nowadays, carrot cakes are sweeter and topped with frosting, especially cream cheese frosting.

Langpannekaker, or "sheet pan cakes," are always served during occasions when there are more mouths to feed. There's something special about serving cake this way, because it's meant to be shared and enjoyed among a gathering of family and friends. It also retains a down-to-earth quality that tells you it's heartfelt and homemade. • *serves 24*

FOR THE CARROT CAKE

5 large eggs, at room temperature

1 cup (240 ml) mild-flavored oil

1 cup (200 g) granulated sugar

1 cup (200 g) dark brown sugar, packed

½ cup (120 ml) buttermilk

2½ cups (300 g) all-purpose flour, sifted

1 tablespoon baking powder

1 teaspoon ground cinnamon

½ teaspoon salt

3 cups (350 g) finely grated carrots

FOR THE CREAM CHEESE FROSTING

8 ounces (225 g) cream cheese

½ cup (112 g) lightly salted butter, at room temperature

1 teaspoon vanilla extract

1 cup (120 g) confectioners' sugar

Carrot ribbons and walnuts, for garnish (optional)

Preheat the oven to 350°F (180°C). Butter a 9 x 13-inch (22.5 x 32.5 cm) baking pan.

For the carrot cake, in a large bowl, whisk together the eggs, oil, granulated sugar, brown sugar, and buttermilk.

In a second large bowl, whisk together the flour, baking powder, cinnamon, and salt. Add the flour mixture to the egg mixture and blend well. Add the carrots and gently fold until evenly incorporated into the batter. Pour the batter into the prepared pan and bake for 25 to 30 minutes or until a toothpick inserted in the center comes out clean. Set aside to cool.

For the cream cheese frosting, beat the cream cheese and butter with a mixer on medium speed until creamy. (If the butter isn't mixing into the frosting, place the frosting, in a heat-proof bowl, over a pot of simmering water and stir frequently until the butter blends in. Don't cook or overheat the frosting; the idea is to just barely melt the butter, so the frosting is fully combined). Add the vanilla and beat to incorporate. Reduce the speed and gradually add the confectioners' sugar until fluffy and smooth.

Spread the cream cheese frosting on top of the cooled cake. Garnish with carrot ribbons and walnuts, if desired, and serve.

Jakten

THE HUNT

The hunt has long been a natural part of human behavior,
as well as a necessity for life and development. In Norway, the ability to provide
oneself with food has always been an essential part of the hunting tradition. This,
paired with Norwegians' strong and well-established affinity for being outdoors,
has forged an important and enduring relationship between the hunter and the
hunted.

Today, the hunt remains strongly embedded in Norwegian culture. However,
the philosophy behind hunting has moved away from a means of survival toward
a wider experience of nature, recreation, and self-sustainability. It's a way to be
physically active and part of a team and a community. It's also a way to connect
with the environment and the food system. The hunt, for many, is a part of their
identity. Perhaps, part of the attraction of being in the woods to hunt is something deep within us, reflecting a natural link to our ancestors.

Wild reindeer and moose moved into Norway following the last Ice Age, and
nomadic tribes followed. These animals provided vital resources, and not only
food, but also clothing and tools. Discoveries of hieroglyphics and animal bones
found on settlements from the Stone Age testify to their importance. The reliance on hunting was critical and a bad hunt could have dire consequences. Thus,
understanding reindeer and moose, especially their habits and movements, was
key to the success of the hunt.

As the population created more permanent settlements, their approach to
and reliance on hunting changed, but even up until the 1950s, there were still
households in Norway subsisting completely, or almost completely, on hunting.
Nowadays, very few Norwegians hunt as an occupation or as a means of income,
but many still spend time and money to go hunting, simply because it improves
their quality of life. In fact, each year in Norway, about 150,000 people hunt, with
ten percent being women.

Unlike most countries, Norway is unique in that hunting has always been
open to everyone, regardless of social class or ethnicity. The hunt was never
reserved for the elite alone, but was rather a right for everyone.

I've had the opportunity to join two hunting teams, one hunting moose and the other hunting grouse. These were extraordinary experiences, and taught me several life lessons. For one, the kill is never guaranteed. It may be the intention, but there is so much more happening around the hunt. It's a holistic process and one in which the journey is just as important as the goal. Many of the hunters I met revealed that some of their fondest memories come from when the group sits quietly next to the fire, surrounded by the forest canopy. It's the conversations, the interactions, and the time spent waiting in the stillness of nature that make for some of the most significant moments, and provide the space to form connections and build relationships.

I also learned that the respect hunters have for one another is the very same respect they have for each and every animal. They're watchful and careful to consider their target and its story before ever taking a shot. Having this kind of genuine connection to the environment and to the food we consume is something to aspire to. Hunting happens, and if we choose to eat meat, we should, at the very least, understand how it's sourced and ensure it's done in the most ethical way possible.

The recipes in this chapter feature a selection of the wild game available in Norway and abroad. Game is usually paired with seasonal berries, mushrooms, nuts, and vegetables. You can always swap elk or deer for moose and reindeer and if you can't find venison, substitute beef, but keep in mind that the taste won't be as rich or earthy. You can also substitute chicken or turkey for pheasant and wild hare. In the introduction, I provide a full list of substitutions you can refer to for all the wild meats mentioned in this chapter. I hope these recipes will serve as an inspiration for utilizing a variety of meats, even if you don't hunt yourself.

Smoked Duck and Barley Salad with Lovage and Plums

SALAT MED RØKT AND, BYGG, LØPSTIKKE OG PLOMME

———————

Duck season begins in early autumn and one of my favorite ways to prepare duck is to smoke it. It's a simple process and makes for fantastic flavor and crispy skin. I tend not to brine duck, but rather pat it dry and generously salt it before it goes in the smoker. A couple of hours later, you get a beautiful bird you can serve as is or added to a dish like this barley salad.

I really love the combination of tastes and textures in this salad, especially the smoky duck with the sweet plum dressing and the chewy, hearty barley. Intensely aromatic lovage rounds everything out, while almonds provide some much-needed crunch. If you can't find lovage, it's possible to substitute celery leaves, but I strongly recommend seeking out lovage. • *serves 4 to 6*

1 cup (200 g) pearl or hulled barley

3 cups plus 1 tablespoon (735 ml) water

1 teaspoon salt, divided

4 plums, pitted

¼ cup (50 g) granulated sugar

¼ cup (60 ml) apple cider vinegar

¼ cup (60 ml) mild-flavored oil

11 ounces (310 g) leafy red lettuce, torn into pieces if large

½ ounce (14 g) lovage leaves, plus more for garnish

¼ cup (30 g) whole almonds, roughly chopped

1 (roughly 5½-pound / 2.5-kg) smoked duck or 4 (roughly 5½-ounce / 156-g) smoked duck breasts, sliced or torn

In a medium, heavy saucepan, combine the barley with 3 cups (720 ml) of the water and ½ teaspoon salt. Bring to a boil and cook for 20 to 45 minutes or until tender—the cook time will vary depending on the type of barley used. Drain and set aside to cool.

Roughly chop 2 of the plums. In a small, heavy saucepan, combine the sugar with the remaining 1 tablespoon water and bring to a gentle simmer, stirring to dissolve the sugar. Add the chopped plum and cook for 10 minutes or until softened and falling apart. Pour through a mesh strainer set over a small bowl, pushing on the plums to release as much juice as possible; discard the solids in the strainer. Add the apple cider vinegar and whisk to combine. While whisking, gradually add the mild-flavored oil and continue whisking the dressing until emulsified. Stir in the remaining ½ teaspoon salt.

Cut the remaining 2 plums into thin wedges and place in a large bowl. Add the cooked barley, red lettuce, lovage, and almonds and toss to combine. Add half the plum dressing and toss again. Arrange the salad on a large serving platter and top with the smoked duck. Garnish with more lovage leaves and serve with the rest of the dressing on the side.

Creamy Pheasant and Wild Mushroom Soup

KREMET SOPPSUPPE MED FASAN

Pheasants are somewhat limited in Norway, and mainly found in the southwestern part of the country, around the Oslofjord. The season for hunting pheasant only runs for two weeks, starting the first day in October. Around this time, I often find myself making a creamy mushroom soup, using wild mushrooms I've just gathered. Pheasant makes for a welcome addition, providing a mild, gamey flavor, but you can easily substitute hen or chicken. • *serves 4*

FOR THE STOCK

1 whole pheasant

1 onion, cut into large pieces

1 carrot, peeled and roughly chopped

1 celery stick, roughly chopped

1 bay leaf

FOR THE MUSHROOM SOUP

2 tablespoons lightly salted butter

1 tablespoon mild-flavored oil

1 onion, finely chopped

2 cloves garlic, finely chopped

1 teaspoon fresh thyme leaves, plus more for garnish

1 pound (450 g) wild mushrooms, such as chanterelles and creminis, sliced

½ teaspoon salt

¼ teaspoon pepper

½ cup (120 ml) heavy cream

For the stock, in a large, heavy pot, add the pheasant, onion, carrot, celery, and bay leaf. Cover with cold water and bring to a boil. Lower the heat, cover, and simmer for about 2 hours or until the meat is falling from the bones. Remove the pheasant and set aside to cool. Pour the stock through a mesh strainer and measure 4¼ cups (1 l) for the soup. Reserve the rest for another use; discard the vegetables and bay leaf.

When the pheasant is cool, pull all the meat from the bones; discard the carcass. Measure 4½ ounces (25 g) pheasant meat and shred any large pieces; reserve the rest for another use.

For the soup, in a large, heavy pot, heat the butter and oil over medium-high heat. Add the onion, garlic, and thyme and sauté for 5 minutes or until the onion is soft and translucent. Add the mushrooms, salt, and pepper and sauté for 5 to 10 minutes or until the mushrooms start to brown and caramelize. Remove from the heat and reserve a handful of mushrooms to use as garnish. Transfer half of the remaining mushrooms to a food processor or blender, add about 2 cups (480 ml) of the reserved pheasant stock and process until smooth. Return the mixture to the pot, add the remaining pheasant stock and cook over medium-low heat for 15 minutes. Add the reserved 4½ ounces (125 g) shredded pheasant meat and cook for 10 minutes or until heated through. Stir in the heavy cream.

Divide the soup among individual bowls, garnish with the reserved sautéed mushrooms and fresh thyme, and serve.

Norwegian Hash

PYTT-I-PANNE

At its core, *pytt-i-panne* is a leftover dish consisting of potatoes, onions, and various meats. It's common across the Nordic region, with each country adding its own twists, and can be as simple or as elegant as you want. I like to add wild meat, as it lends depth of flavor. This is also a perfect meal for when you're on a hunt, because you can easily prepare the ingredients beforehand, have them in your sack, and fry everything over an open fire when ready. Feel free to add various vegetables, sausages, or whatever else you might have lying around to make this dish your own. A side of pickles or pickled beets adds a welcome acidity. • *serves 4*

4 tablespoons mild-flavored oil

4 tablespoons (56 g) lightly salted butter, divided

2 large onions, cut into ½-inch (1.25 cm) cubes

1½ pounds (680 g) potatoes, cut into ½-inch (1.25 cm) cubes

⅓ pound (150 g) sweet potatoes, peeled, cut into ½-inch (1.25 cm) cubes

1 pound (450 g) leftover cooked moose, reindeer, or venison, cut into pieces

A few sprigs fresh thyme

½ teaspoon salt

¼ teaspoon pepper

4 large eggs

In a large frying pan, heat the oil and 2 tablespoons of the butter over medium-high heat. Add the onions, potatoes, and sweet potatoes and stir to coat in the butter and oil. Add the leftover cooked meat, thyme, salt, and pepper and stir to combine. Lower the heat, cover, and cook, stirring occasionally, for about 20 minutes or until the potatoes are soft and the hash is nicely browned. Season to taste with salt and pepper then transfer to a serving bowl and keep warm.

In the same pan, melt the remaining 2 tablespoons butter over medium heat until lightly foaming. Gently crack the eggs into the pan, season to taste with salt and pepper, and cook for 2 minutes or until the whites begin to set. Carefully flip the eggs over to avoid breaking the yolks and continue cooking for a few more seconds or longer for less runny yolks. Slide the fried eggs on top of the hash. Serve immediately.

Venison Stuffed Cabbage Rolls

KÅLRULETTER MED HJORT

Cabbage rolls are a classic dish, and for many of us, reminiscent of childhood memories. Various meat and cabbage rolls are made around the world—I remember my mother making her own version—but in Norway, they're typically made with pork, and served with a tomato or white sauce.

I really like the use of venison in this dish. I'll even go so far as to say these are the best cabbage rolls I've ever tasted. Though venison is lean, these cabbage rolls are so incredibly flavorful and juicy that they don't need any sauce. Using a leafy cabbage, instead of white cabbage, gives the rolls a softer texture that's easier to chew. It also makes separating the cabbage leaves a whole lot easier. • *serves 4 to 6*

1¾ pounds (800 g) ground venison

2½ teaspoons salt

1 large egg

1 clove garlic, minced

2 tablespoons cornstarch

1 teaspoon black pepper

1 teaspoon ground nutmeg

1 teaspoon dried thyme

1½ cups (360 ml) milk

1 large leafy green cabbage, such as savoy or summer cabbage

2 tablespoons lightly salted butter, cut into pieces

In a food processor, combine the venison and salt and pulse for 1 minute. Add the egg, garlic, cornstarch, pepper, nutmeg, and thyme and pulse until well blended. While the machine is running, gradually add the milk and process until a smooth paste forms. Set aside.

Fill a large bowl with ice water and bring a large pot of salted water to a boil.

Carefully pull 12 leaves from the cabbage, keeping the leaves intact. Using tongs, carefully plunge the cabbage into the boiling water, 1 leaf at a time, and blanch for about 30 seconds then immediately plunge into the bowl of ice water. Drain the cabbage. Measure ¼ cup (60 ml) of the cabbage boiling water and reserve for later use; discard the rest.

Preheat the oven to 425°F (220°C).

Place 2 large spoonfuls of the meat mixture in the center of 1 cabbage leaf then fold both sides of the cabbage leaf over the meat. Roll the bottom of the leaf up to form a rolled bundle then place, seam-side down, in a 7 x 11-inch (18 x 28 cm), or similar, baking dish. Continue making cabbage rolls with the remaining meat and cabbage and arrange, side by side, in 2 rows, in the baking dish. Pour the reserved cabbage boiling water over the cabbage rolls and top with a couple pieces of butter. Cover with foil and bake for 25 to 30 minutes or until the meat is cooked through.

Serve the cabbage rolls with the juices from the pan.

Venison Stew
with Wild Mushrooms

VILTGRYTE

Viltgryte, which translates to "wild stew," is made with wild meat, typically moose, reindeer, or venison. It's a classic hunting season dish, and features flavors from the forest, such as juniper berries, wild mushrooms, and wild berries. Rich and creamy, viltgryte is more like a gravy than a stew, and should always be served with a side of potatoes. If you can't find lingonberries, substitute red currants, huckleberries, or bilberries. • *serves 4*

2 tablespoons mild-flavored oil, plus more as needed

1¾ pounds (800 g) venison steak, cut into chunks

3 tablespoons lightly salted butter, divided

1 large onion, finely chopped

½ pound (225 g) chanterelles or other wild mushrooms

6 dried juniper berries, crushed

½ teaspoon salt

¼ teaspoon pepper

2 cups (480 ml) game or beef stock

½ cup (120 ml) heavy cream

3 tablespoons sour cream

½ pound (225 g) Brussels sprouts, ends trimmed and outer leaves removed

Lingonberries (optional)

Fresh thyme leaves

In a large, heavy saucepan, heat the oil over medium-high heat. Working in batches and adding more oil as needed, sear the venison, turning, for 2 minutes or until brown on all sides. Transfer to a bowl and set aside.

In the same saucepan, melt 2 tablespoons of the butter over medium-high heat. Add the onions and cook for 5 minutes or until just softened. Add the mushrooms, juniper berries, salt, and pepper and sauté for 5 to 10 minutes or until the mushrooms are soft and most of their juices evaporate. Return the venison and any juices from the bowl to the saucepan. Add the stock and bring to a boil then lower the heat, cover, and simmer gently for 1 hour or until the meat is tender. Stir in the heavy cream and sour cream and bring to a gentle boil. Continue cooking, uncovered, for 10 to 15 minutes or until slightly thickened.

While the stew is simmering, in a large, heavy frying pan, melt the remaining 1 tablespoon butter over medium-high heat. Add the Brussels sprouts and a pinch of salt and shake the pan. Lower the heat to medium, cover, and cook, shaking the pan occasionally, for 10 minutes or until the sprouts begin to crisp and look slightly charred.

Divide the stew among bowls then top with Brussels sprouts and sprinkle with lingonberries and thyme. Serve with boiled or mashed potatoes.

Rowanberry Jelly

ROGNEBÆRGELÉ

In autumn, clusters of vibrant red and orange berries cover the rowan trees, also known as mountain ash trees. With their branches bowing under the weight of the berry blossoms, the trees signal that the seasons are changing, and while some dismiss them as food for the birds, those red and orange berries can be used to enhance so many dishes, especially those made with wild meats.

Here in Norway, you'll find rowanberries are typically used to make jelly. Though incredibly bitter and off-putting when raw, if cooked down and sweetened, the berries turn mellow and bright. Once tamed, that initial bitterness counters the sugar, resulting in a beautiful balance of the two. This jelly makes a great accompaniment to wild game, and is often stirred into autumn stews. • *makes about 2 quarts (2 l)*

2¼ pounds (1 kg) rowanberries, washed
1¾ pounds (800 g) apples, cored

About 5 to 6 cups (1 to 1.2 kg) granulated sugar

In a large, heavy pot, combine the rowanberries and apples with just enough cold water to cover. Bring to a boil then lower the heat and simmer, stirring only once or twice, for about 30 minutes or until the berries and apples are soft and release their juices. Strain through a cheesecloth or jelly bag, set over a large bowl, and let it drip on its own for at least 1 hour. To keep the jelly clear, do not squeeze out the juice; discard the fruit.

Measure the amount of juice then calculate ½ cup (100 g) granulated sugar for every ½ cup (120 ml) juice. In a clean, large, heavy pot, combine the juice and sugar over medium-high heat, stirring until the sugar dissolves, and bring to a boil. Continue boiling, skimming any scum from the top, for about 10 minutes or until set. To test, spoon a little jam on a cold plate and push the spoon across it. If the jam wrinkles, it's ready. If not, boil 5 to 10 more minutes. Once ready, transfer the jam to sterilized glass jars with lids and seal. Leave undisturbed for 48 hours for a good set. When sealed properly, the jam can last up to a year unopened. When opened, it should last up to 2 weeks in the refrigerator.

Moose Burger with Crispy Caramelized Onions, Forest Berry Relish, and Root Vegetable Chips

ELGBURGER

The Norwegian *elg,* or "moose," in English, is known fondly in Norway as *skogens konge,* which translates to "king of the forest." The title is fitting, as their very being is a symbol of the wild and the majesty and dignity of the landscape.

I wanted to create a burger that truly captures these forest kings and this is it. The patty is 100 percent moose meat, cloaked in melted cheese, and topped with a crown of golden onions and forest berry relish. Moose is extremely lean, so it's important to add a little fat and not overcook the meat. If moose isn't available, try using venison, reindeer, elk, or beef. Serve root vegetable chips on the side to make this a complete meal. • *serves 4*

FOR THE CRISPY ONIONS

1 tablespoon mild-flavored oil

1 large yellow onion, cut into thin rings

⅛ teaspoon salt

FOR THE FOREST BERRY RELISH

1 tablespoon mild-flavored oil

2 large shallots, diced

2 cups (180 g) mixed forest berries, such as blackberries, bilberries, raspberries, and currants

2 tablespoons granulated sugar

1 tablespoon freshly squeezed lemon juice

¼ teaspoon dried chili flakes

FOR THE ROOT VEGETABLE CHIPS

About 6¼ cups (1.5 l) vegetable oil

2 large parsnips, peeled into ribbons

2 large beets, peeled and cut into very thin slices

Flaky salt

FOR THE BURGERS

1⅓ pounds (600 g) ground moose meat

2 tablespoons plus 1 teaspoon mild-flavored oil

1 teaspoon salt

Cheese, such as Norwegian *hvit geitost* or Gouda, sliced

4 hamburger buns

Lettuce leaves, for serving

For the crispy onions, in a large, heavy pan, heat the oil over medium-high heat. Add the yellow onions, lower to medium heat, season with the salt, and sauté for about 20 minutes or until darker in color and a little crispy. Keep warm.

For the forest berry relish, in a small, heavy saucepan, heat the oil over medium-high heat. Add the shallots and sauté for 2 minutes or until soft and golden. Stir in the berries, sugar, lemon juice, and chili flakes then lower the heat and simmer for about 10 minutes or until the relish is thick. Remove from the heat and let cool.

Line a large plate with paper towels.

For the root vegetable chips, heat the oil in a large, heavy saucepan over medium-high heat. When you can drop in a parsnip ribbon and it begins to sizzle, the oil is hot enough. Working in batches, carefully place the parsnip ribbons in the oil and fry, turning occasionally, for about 1 minute or until golden. Transfer to the paper towel–lined plate and immediately sprinkle with salt. Repeat with the remaining parsnips then work in batches to fry the beets, turning occasionally, for 3 to 4 minutes or until the edges begin to curl. Transfer to the paper towel–lined plate and immediately sprinkle with salt.

For the burgers, in a medium bowl, gently combine the ground moose meat and 1 tablespoon plus 1 teaspoon oil (if substituting beef, omit the oil). Form the meat into 4 equal-size patties, pressing your thumb into the middle of each to make a little indentation. Season each patty with ¼ teaspoon salt, sprinkling it on the tops and bottoms.

In a large, heavy pan, heat the remaining 1 tablespoon oil over high heat. Add the patties and cook for 3 to 4 minutes then flip and cook for 2 minutes or until medium rare. Divide the cheese among the patties, cover, and cook for 1 minute or just until the cheese melts—moose and other lean meats overcook easily, so I recommend a total cooking time of 6 to 7 minutes. If using beef, you may need to cook longer to reach your desired doneness.

Arrange some lettuce on the bottom of each bun then top with a patty, followed by crispy onions and forest berry relish. Finish with the bun tops and serve with the root vegetable chips.

Reindeer Stew with Samisk Bread

REINSDYRGRYTE MED SAMISK BRØD

The Sami are the northernmost indigenous people of Norway, Sweden, Finland, and Russia's Kola Peninsula. Reindeer is their livelihood and staple food, as well as berries and fish. The Sami follow a "nose to tail" diet, in which every part of the animal is utilized and nothing is wasted—not even the hooves.

The Sami make an incredible bread that's traditionally cooked over a stone or dry griddle next to the fire. The bread is slightly sweet, and when cooked with a little oil, the flavor really shines. It's a yeast-based bread, and typically served with meats and fish, or alongside stews, such as the traditional reindeer-based *bidos*. I was inspired by this, as well as the fry breads and stews I grew up eating in the U.S., but my version features reindeer stew served on top of the bread, rather than alongside. If you can't find reindeer (also known as caribou) meat, make this hearty dish with venison, moose, elk, or even beef if unable to access game. • *serves 4*

FOR THE LINGONBERRY CHUTNEY

1 cup (100 g) frozen lingonberries or cranberries, thawed

½ large red onion, diced

1 tablespoon dark brown sugar

1 tablespoon white vinegar

Juice of ½ lemon

FOR THE BREAD

½ cup (120 ml) milk

1 ounce (25 g) fresh yeast or ⅓ ounce (8.5 g) active dry yeast

½ cup (120 ml) lukewarm water

2 tablespoons lightly salted butter

1 tablespoon Norwegian dark syrup or light molasses

2¾ cups (330 g) all-purpose flour, sifted

3 tablespoons plus 1 teaspoon (25 g) whole-wheat flour, sifted

3 tablespoons vegetable oil, plus more as needed

FOR THE STEW

1 teaspoon salt

1 teaspoon ground coriander

½ teaspoon garlic powder

½ teaspoon onion powder

½ teaspoon juniper berries, crushed

½ teaspoon white pepper

¼ teaspoon black pepper

1 pound (450 g) reindeer meat, cut into small pieces

2 tablespoons mild-flavored oil

1 onion, diced

2 tablespoons lightly salted butter

1 clove garlic, minced

1 carrot, peeled and diced

2 medium potatoes, diced

1 tablespoon all-purpose flour

2 cups (480 ml) venison or chicken stock

Grated semi-hard mild cheese, sour cream, and chopped fresh flat-leaf parsley, for serving

For the lingonberry chutney, in a small bowl, combine the lingonberries, red onion, brown sugar, vinegar, and lemon juice and set aside. If substituting with cranberries, roughly chop them before combining with the other ingredients.

For the bread, in small saucepan, heat the milk over medium heat until just warm. Pour into a large bowl, add the yeast, and whisk until combined. Add the water, along with the butter and dark syrup, followed by the all-purpose and whole-wheat flours and combine. On a floured surface, knead the dough for about 10 minutes or until smooth. Return to the bowl, cover with a tea towel, and let rise in a warm spot for about 30 minutes or until doubled in size.

While the dough is rising, start the stew. In a small bowl, combine the salt, coriander, garlic powder, onion powder, juniper berries, and white and black pepper. In a large bowl, toss the reindeer meat with 1 tablespoon of the seasoning mixture.

In a large, heavy pan, heat the oil over high heat. Add the onion and ½ tablespoon of the spice mixture and sauté, stirring, for 5 minutes or until the onions start sticking to the bottom of the pan. Add the butter and as soon as it melts, add the reindeer meat and cook, stirring occasionally, for 5 minutes. Add the garlic and cook for 1 minute then add the carrot, potatoes, and the remaining spice mixture and cook for 2 minutes. Add the flour and cook, stirring, for 2 minutes. Add the venison or chicken stock and bring to a boil then lower the heat and simmer for 15 minutes or until the vegetables are soft. Set the heat as low as possible to keep the stew warm while you finish the bread.

Divide the dough into 4 equal portions and shape each portion into a flat 5-inch (13 cm) round disc.

In a large, heavy pan, heat the vegetable oil over medium-high heat. Add 1 disc of dough and fry, flipping once, about 1 minute per side or until golden brown. Repeat with the remaining dough, adding more oil as necessary.

Place the breads on individual plates or in bowls and top with stew. Garnish with lingonberry chutney, grated cheese, sour cream, and parsley and serve immediately.

Walnut and Rye-Encrusted Grouse with Buttery Blackcurrant Sauce

RYPE MED SOLBÆR

Grouse is one of the more popular birds hunted in Norway, and there are two kinds, *lirype* and *fjellrype*. Typically, grouse is seared like steak or slow-cooked in a creamy sauce. In this recipe, I marinate the breasts in buttermilk before coating them with crushed walnuts and rye flour and then searing them. I like serving grouse with a simple sauce made with blackcurrants, which have an earthy taste that's both tart and sweet. If you can't find fresh blackcurrants, look for frozen, or use fresh or frozen blackberries and thaw before using. • *serves 4*

FOR THE GROUSE

4 boneless grouse breasts

1 cup (240 ml) buttermilk

½ cup (50 g) walnuts

½ cup (60 g) fine rye flour

½ teaspoon salt

¼ teaspoon pepper

Pinch ground nutmeg

3 tablespoons lightly salted butter, plus more as needed

FOR THE BLACKCURRANT SAUCE

2 tablespoons lightly salted butter

½ tablespoon granulated sugar

1 cup (240 ml) fresh blackcurrants

In a resealable plastic bag, combine the grouse breasts and buttermilk. Seal the bag and marinate in the refrigerator for at least 1 hour.

In a food processor, pulse the walnuts until finely ground. Add the rye flour, salt, pepper, and nutmeg and pulse once or twice just to combine then transfer to a large plate. Take the grouse breasts out of the bag and dredge them in the walnut mixture, making sure they're evenly coated.

In a large, heavy pan, heat the butter over medium-high heat until foaming—if the butter doesn't completely coat the pan, add more. Add the grouse breasts and cook, turning once, 2 to 3 minutes per side or until golden brown. Transfer the breasts to a platter and let rest for 10 minutes.

While the breasts are resting, make the blackcurrant sauce. In a small saucepan, heat the butter over medium-high heat until foaming. Add the sugar and stir until dissolved. Add the blackcurrants and cook, gently tossing so they stay intact, for about 15 seconds or until just softened and releasing their juices. Remove from the heat and immediately serve alongside the grouse.

Hare Fricassee

HAREFRIKASSÉ

Norwegian fricassee, notably with French roots, is a long-standing tradition in Norway. It's a classic dish that's typically made with lamb, veal, chicken, or hen, but if you can get your hands on hare (wild or domesticated), I think it works particularly well in fricassee. Hare hunting is Norway's oldest *sportsjakt*, or "sport hunting," and arrived from the continent in the sixteen hundreds. When slow cooked, hare meat is tender and has a delicious, slightly gamey flavor. Feel free to substitute with chicken or turkey if hare is not readily available. • *serves 4 to 6*

1 (3-pound / 1.3-kg) hare, skinned, cleaned, and jointed

1 teaspoon salt, divided

½ cup plus 1 tablespoon (125 g) lightly salted butter, divided

1 onion, roughly chopped

2 bay leaves

Zest and juice of 1 lemon

3 to 4 carrots, peeled and sliced

1 large leek, washed and thinly sliced

1 celery root, peeled and diced

½ cup (60 g) all-purpose flour, sifted

½ cup (120 ml) heavy cream

Pepper

Season the hare with ½ teaspoon salt.

In a large, heavy pot, heat 3 tablespoons of the butter over medium-high heat. Add the hare pieces and cook, turning, for 2 to 3 minutes or until brown on all sides. Transfer the hare pieces to a plate and set aside. Add the onion to the pan and sauté, occasionally scraping the bottom of the pot, for 1 minute. Return the hare pieces to the pot. Add enough cold water to cover, along with the bay leaves and lemon zest, and bring to a boil. Lower the heat, cover, and simmer for 1½ hours or until the meat is falling from the bones. Remove the hare pieces and set aside to cool. When the hare is cool, pull all the meat from the bones; discard the bones.

Pour the stock through a mesh strainer into a clean, large, heavy pot; discard the onion and bay leaves. Bring to a boil then add the carrots, leek, and celery root and cook for about 10 minutes or until tender. Transfer the vegetables to a bowl and set aside. Measure 3 cups (720 ml) of stock and set aside for later; reserve the rest for another use.

In a large, heavy saucepan, heat the remaining 6 tablespoons (84 g) butter over medium heat. Add the flour and cook, whisking for about 2 minutes. Slowly whisk in the reserved 3 cups (720 ml) stock, along with the remaining ½ teaspoon salt and cook for about 8 minutes or until the sauce is thick. Stir in the heavy cream and remove from the heat. Stir the hare and vegetables into the sauce and season to taste with salt and pepper.

Divide the fricassee among bowls. Finish each serving with a squeeze of lemon juice, and serve with a side of boiled potatoes.

Stabburet

THE STORAGE HOUSE

The *stabbur* stands out among the other farm buildings, with stories reflecting its purpose carved into the wear and tear on its wooden framework. For the generations working and living on these farms, the stabbur has been an incredibly valuable structure, not only because it was a place to store and keep food from spoiling, but also because that food was an important commodity for the livelihood of the families living there.

The origin of the word stabbur is unknown, though it may stem from *bu,* meaning "storage house," *bur,* meaning "house," or *stavbur,* which refers to a house built in *stavverk,* the oldest wood-building method in Norway. The stabbur was originally one level and built directly on the ground, but it was later raised on wood platforms and placed atop stones. This was to keep rats and mice away and to help air circulate around the floorboards so the humidity would stay low. The platforms were designed and carved in a way to prevent small animals from climbing into the stabbur. There was also a large space between the top of the steps and the entrance for the same purpose.

For centuries, the stabbur played a vital role in the storage of food. It was built to stock flour and grains, especially barley and oats, as well as flatbreads and cured meats and fish. It was also where farmers kept the grain seeds for the next year's planting. If there was a second floor, that's where flour and grains were stored in large wooden bins. Smoked and salted meats were hung on hooks from the lower ceiling, while salted fish and the fat from the cured meats was stored in closed wooden barrels. Flatbreads were stacked high on top of each other, and were meant to last an entire year. The doorway was often used as a cutting surface, a place to stabilize cured meats, so pieces could be cut off as needed. If you look closely at the doorframes on a stabbur, they'll often reveal slashes in the wood, echoing this practice.

The stabbur was one of the few buildings on the farm with a lock. The value of food was so high, the stabbur acted almost as a bank, protecting the family's commodities. Some families even placed large, flat stones on the floorboards to prevent thieves from drilling holes to get inside. The housewife was the one who took care of the key, which was symbolic of her status and position on the farm.

A bell hanging from the top of the stabbur, in its own little tower, was another status symbol. Called the *matklokka,* or "food clock," among other names, this bell was found at many of the larger farms, and was about more than prestige; it was also a sign of practicality. The bell was used to announce when food was ready and it was time to take a break. On larger farms, this was especially helpful, as workers were often spread across large expanses of land. The bells were used throughout spring, summer, and autumn, and became a sign of the coming of spring, when chimes would reverberate across the region following a long winter.

The stabbur has had an enormous impact on Norway's food culture, which is why I chose to dedicate an entire chapter to the types of food stored here. The recipes highlight dishes made from these building block ingredients, including flatbreads, grains, and cured meats. While curing meat is time consuming, it's not difficult and doesn't require a lot of ingredients. Many Norwegians continue to make their own cured meats at home, which allows them to tailor the flavors and textures to suit their own preferences. It takes a little practice to gain an intuitive sense of when the meat is finished curing and to one's liking, but the results are worth it. If you're not able to source meat directly from a farmer, the cuts used for the leg of lamb and lamb ribs will probably need to be special ordered from a butcher. For dishes using cured meats as an ingredient, you can purchase these at any supermarket. The other ingredients should be easy to acquire and if you're not making your own flatbread, substitutes can also be purchased.

Flatbread Cereal with Cherry Compote

BRØDSOLL

This traditional, everyday dish highlights the simplicity of cooking, as well as the ingenuity of taking a recipe and changing it to reflect the ingredients on hand. *Brødsoll* is Norway's version of milk toast—bread with milk—with pieces of flatbread soaking up sweetened or soured milk to create a simple cereal.

Brødsoll used to be a common farm meal, and was served either warm or cold. It's not eaten as often anymore, which is a shame, because it's so simple to make, and is a good base for a variety of toppings. You can serve brødsoll traditionally, with a sprinkling of sugar on top, or add fruit, as I have here. • *serves 4*

2 cups fresh cherries, pitted

¼ cup (60 ml) water

2 tablespoons granulated sugar

4 multigrain flatbreads

Whole milk, buttermilk, kefir, or yogurt

In a medium, heavy saucepan, combine the cherries, water, and sugar and bring to a boil. Lower the heat, cover, and simmer for about 20 minutes or until the compote is thick. Set aside to cool.

Break the flatbread into large pieces and divide among bowls. Pour a generous amount of milk, kefir, buttermilk, or yogurt over the flatbread and top with the cherry compote. Serve immediately—the longer the flatbread sits, the more it will soften and lose its texture.

Potato Flatbread

POTETFLATBRØD

There are many variations of flatbread across Norway, but most are made with a combination of grains, such as barley, oat, and wheat. And ever since the introduction of potatoes in the eighteen hundreds, those have been used as well.

This versatile recipe comes from Liv Jorunn and Ingebjørg from Rollag. It contains a mixture of grains and potatoes, which gives it incredible flavor. Making flatbread takes time, so it's good to have some help and make a day of it. The result will be a stack of flatbreads ready to be eaten or stored for a long time. If you use a Norwegian griddle called a *takke,* you can make large flatbreads, but if you use a large frying pan instead, you'll have to make smaller ones. I sometimes make just a third of the recipe if I'm alone in the kitchen, so feel free to scale back or make the whole batch.

makes 30 to 60 flatbreads

5½ pounds (2.5 kg) starchy potatoes, such as Beate, Kerr's Pink, or russet

2½ teaspoons salt

1¼ cups (150 g) whole-wheat flour

1½ cups (200 g) coarse rye flour

9 cups (1.1 kg) all-purpose flour, sifted, plus more as needed

3 cups (360 g) oat flour, plus more as needed

In a large pot, cover the potatoes with cold salted water and bring to a boil. Lower the heat and simmer for 10 minutes or until the potatoes are barely tender when pierced with a knife. Peel the potatoes and push through a ricer twice into a large bowl. Add the salt, along with the whole-wheat and rye flours. Stir to combine, cover, and refrigerate overnight.

In the morning, divide the dough into 3 equal portions and place 1 portion in a stand mixer fitted with the dough hook attachment. With the mixer on low, gradually add 3 cups (360 g) of the all-purpose flour and 1 cup (120 g) of the oat flour. As you're adding flour, occasionally turn the mixer off and use your hands to push the dough down. Continue mixing, adding a little more of the all-purpose and oat flours as needed, while maintaining a roughly 3 to 1 ratio of all-purpose to oat flour, for 8 to 10 minutes or until the dough is soft and elastic. Repeat with the remaining 2 portions of dough and the remaining all-purpose and oat flours.

On a well-floured surface, divide each portion of dough into 10 balls, about 4 ounces (120 g) each. If using a large frying pan instead of a takke, divide each portion into 20 balls, about 2 ounces (60 g) each. Using an indented or regular rolling pin and adding more all-purpose flour as needed, roll out each ball of dough into a large, thin, even circle, about 16½ inches (42 cm) in diameter or half that size if using a large frying pan. Using a soft-bristled brush, dust any excess flour from both sides of the dough.

Heat a takke or large frying pan over medium heat. Add 1 round of dough and cook, flipping a few times, for about 10 minutes or until golden and stiff—the flatbreads will firm up slightly as they cool. Repeat with the remaining rounds of dough. Serve immediately or let the flatbreads cool then stack and store in a cool, dry place for up to a year.

Cured Lamb Ribs with Rutabaga Mash

PINNEKJØTT MED KÅLRABISTAPPE

Pinnekjøtt, a classic dish that emerged from the need for preserving meat and originally served for celebratory occasions, is now mostly reserved for Christmas Eve. It's made with lamb or sheep ribs that are cured and then hung to dry for several weeks, before being cooked, which means this dish requires some planning ahead.

This recipe comes from my father-in-law, Asle, who is from Ona. It's unique in that the cured and dried ribs are boiled rather than steamed, before being baked. I find this makes the meat exceptionally tender and also less salty. It's arguably one of the best pinnekjøtt meals you'll ever eat. It's tradition to serve the ribs with a rutabaga mash, plus boiled potatoes and a shot of aquavit to finish it all off. When making the rutabaga mash, you can swap the optional heavy cream for juices from the pan used to bake the ribs. • *serves 4*

FOR THE LAMB

6¾ pounds (3 kg) lamb ribs

9 ounces (250 g) fine salt

1 tablespoon granulated sugar

4 tablespoons (56 g) lightly salted butter

FOR THE MASHED RUTABAGA

1 large rutabaga, peeled and cut into small pieces

4 small starchy potatoes, peeled and cut into quarters

3½ tablespoons (50 g) lightly salted butter

About ⅓ cup (80 ml) heavy cream (optional)

Salt and white pepper

For the lamb, place the ribs in a large container. Using your hands, work the salt and sugar into the ribs, completely covering the entire surface. Cover and refrigerate or let stand in a cool place for 2 to 3 days, depending on the size—the larger the ribs the longer it needs to cure. The meat will release its juices, so several times a day, spoon any liquid in the container over the meat.

After 2 to 3 days, using your hands, brush off any excess salt and sugar. Hang the ribs in a dark, mostly dry, and well-ventilated space—46°F to 54°F (8°C to 12°C) is ideal—for 5 to 8 weeks, depending on the size of the rack. Determining when the lamb is ready comes with experience. When you knock on the rack, it should sound hollow, which is a sign that it's completely dry. At this point, you can proceed with cooking the ribs or freezing them. If freezing, cut the ribs as instructed below then place in a freezer bag, seal, and freeze for up to 6 months. When ready to cook frozen ribs, let them thaw 24 hours before baking.

The day before you plan to cook the ribs, use a strong, sharp knife to cut the rack into individual pieces. Place the ribs in a large, heavy pot, cover with cold water, and let soak at room temperature for 12 hours.

Drain the ribs and return to the pot—the ribs should fit snugly in the bottom. Add just enough cold water to cover the ribs then cover the pot and bring to a gentle simmer. Continue simmering for 2 to 3 hours or until the meat pulls easily off the bone.

Preheat the oven to 425°F (220°C).

Transfer the ribs to a large roasting pan and cover with foil to keep warm. Reserve the water from the pot and let cool slightly. As the water cools, scum and fat will rise to the top. Remove the foil from the roasting pan and pour the scum and fat over the ribs. Scatter the butter on top, but do not return the foil to the pan. Bake, flipping the ribs over about halfway through and occasionally basting them with their juices, for 15 to 20 minutes or until the ribs are browned and their fat is slightly crispy.

For the rutabaga mash, in a large, heavy saucepan, cover the rutabaga and potatoes with cold salted water and bring to a boil. Lower the heat and simmer until the vegetables are tender when pierced with a knife. Drain the vegetables and transfer to a large bowl. Add the butter, and heavy cream, if using, and mash until combined. Season to taste with salt and pepper.

Serve the ribs warm with the rutabaga mash, some boiled potatoes, and the juices from the pan.

Cured Leg of Lamb

FENALÅR

———————

There's nothing quite like a slice of *fenalår*—salted, dried, and cured leg of lamb—especially when it's homemade. I distinctly remember my husband and his family presenting it to me for the first time, with a large knife stuck in for each person to slice off a piece. Fenalår has grown on me over the years and I look forward to making it every autumn, just in time for winter. It's a lengthy process, but definitely worth it. Fenalår goes well with so many dishes and is a great substitute for other cured meats like prosciutto or bresaola. • *makes 1 large cured leg of lamb*

FOR DRY SALTING THE LAMB

1⅔ pounds (750 g) coarse salt

2 tablespoons granulated sugar

1 (6¾-pound / 3-kg) bone-in leg of lamb

FOR BRINING THE LAMB

2⅔ gallons (10 l) cold water

7¾ pounds (3.5 kg) fine salt

⅓ cup plus 1 teaspoon (70 g) granulated sugar

For dry salting the lamb, in a large bowl, combine the coarse salt and 2 tablespoons sugar. Place the leg of lamb in a large plastic container and cover with the salt and sugar mixture. Using your hands, work the mixture into the meat, making sure to completely cover the entire surface. Cover and refrigerate for 2 days.

After 2 days, brine the lamb: Using your hands, brush any excess salt and sugar off the lamb and into the container. Set the lamb aside. Pour the water into the container, add the fine salt and ⅓ cup plus 1 teaspoon (70 g) sugar and mix until dissolved. Place the lamb back in the container with the brine, making sure it's completely submerged—you can place a weight on top to keep it submerged. Cover and refrigerate for 3 days.

After 3 days, remove the lamb from the brine and thread a metal hook or strong twine through the anklebone. Hang in a dark, mostly dry, and well-ventilated space—46°F to 54°F (8°C to 12°C) is ideal. Determining when the lamb is ready comes with experience. It should be ready when its initial weight is reduced by 30 to 40 percent, which should take 2 to 3 months.

To serve, cut thin slices from the lower end of the leg, working upwards toward the thigh. The meat continues to dry as it's stored, so it's better to start eating the thinner parts of the leg first. You can also serve fenalår with porridges, soups, and salads or even fried on top of ice cream. To store, place uncovered in a cupboard or dark and dry area for about a month. When all the meat is gone, save the bone to make stock.

Cured Eye of Round

SPEKET LÅRTUNGE

———————

Eye of round is often overlooked, because it's a very lean cut and can be tough if not cooked properly. Curing, however, results in a delicious and flavorful meat. While curing typically involves a little trial and error, this recipe is quite forgiving so it's a good one to start with if you're new to curing. · *makes 1 cured eye of round*

1 (1 to 2 pounds / 450 to 900 g) beef or moose eye of round

About 3 to 6 cups (750 g to 1.5 kg) coarse salt

About ¼ cup (60 ml) Norwegian dark syrup or light molasses

Pat the eye of round dry and place snuggly in a rimmed container. Add enough coarse salt to completely cover the eye of round and use your hands to work it into the meat, covering the entire surface. Cover and refrigerate or place in a cool place to cure. The amount of time required for curing not only depends on the weight of the meat, but also on the age of the animal and here are some guidelines to follow:

A young calf – about 1 day in salt
Adolescent animal – about 1½ to 2 days in salt
Adult animal – about 2½ to 3 days in salt

After the salting period, remove the eye of round and use your hands to brush off all the salt.

Place the eye of round in a large bowl, add enough dark syrup to coat, and use your hands to work it into the meat, covering the entire surface.

Using a sharp knife, make a small hole through the eye of round, about 1 inch (2.5 cm) below the top. Push a piece of kitchen twine, long enough to hang the meat, through the hole. Tie the ends of the twine and hang the eye of round from a hook or nail in a dark, mostly dry, and well-ventilated space—46°F to 54°F (8°C to 12°C) is ideal.

After 5 days, cut the eye of round in half and cut off a slice to taste. It should be a nice burgundy color in the middle. If you want it a little drier, hang for up to 2 more days, checking it every day until it has the desired texture. The eye of round can be stored in an airtight container and kept at room temperature for up to 1 month, although it will dry out the longer it sits.

Slice the eye of round and serve on flatbread with butter or with lingonberries stirred into sour cream. It's also good with potato salad and scrambled eggs. You can even cut a thick slice and grill it over the fire.

Shaved Cured Pork with Pickled Fennel and Strawberries

SALAT MED SPEKESKINKE

It's quite a sight to see a stabbur lined with rows and rows of hanging pig thighs (*spekeskinke*) that have been curing for anywhere from three months to over a year. It feels like walking into a market, where the butcher is just waiting to cut off a thin slice and enthusiastically explain the maturity, flavors, and tenderness of the meat, as well as the source of the pigs, which would no doubt be local.

In the summer, paper-thin slices of spekeskinke turn a salad of fresh strawberries, pickled fennel, and hazelnuts into something extraordinary. I like to serve this as an appetizer or as part of a light meal with other dishes. Start this dish one day ahead so the fennel has time to pickle. *serves 4*

1 cup (240 ml) distilled white vinegar

½ cup (120 ml) water

¼ cup (50 g) granulated sugar

½ teaspoon salt

1 to 2 fennel bulbs, trimmed and thinly sliced

7 ounces (200 g) thinly sliced cured pork

1 cup (145 g) strawberries, hulled and quartered

¼ small red onion, thinly sliced

1 ounce (28 g) aged white cheese made of goat's milk, shaved with a vegetable peeler

¼ cup (26 g) hazelnuts, roughly chopped

Olive oil

Butterfly sorrel or chives, for garnish

In a small, heavy saucepan, bring the distilled white vinegar, water, sugar, and salt to a boil, stirring to dissolve. Remove from the heat and set aside.

Place the fennel strips in a 1-pint (500 ml) glass jar. Add the brine, making sure the fennel is completely covered and let cool to room temperature. Place a lid on the jar and refrigerate overnight.

Arrange the slices of cured pork on a large platter. Top with the pickled fennel, strawberries, red onion, cheese, and hazelnuts. Drizzle with olive oil, garnish with butterfly sorrel or chives, and serve.

Pan-Fried Pears Wrapped in Cured Pork with Honey and Pink Peppercorns

PÆRE MED SPEKESKINKE

Salty, rich cured meat and fresh sweet fruit are a natural and balanced pairing. When pan-fried together, the crispy texture of the meat against the warm, softened flesh of the fruit brings this pairing to a whole new level. I enjoy serving these special bundles, because they're flavorful, fresh, and quick to pull together. If you prefer, you can substitute another cured meat, fenalår (lamb). *serves 4 to 6*

4 large pears

8 to 16 pieces thinly sliced cured pork

2 tablespoons lightly salted butter, for frying

Flaky salt

Crushed pink peppercorns

Runny honey

Cut the pears lengthwise in half. Carefully remove the cores and seeds, but leave the stems. Wrap each pear half with 1 to 2 slices of the cured pork and press the fat of the meat together to keep from it from falling off the pear.

In a large, heavy frying pan, heat the butter over medium-high heat until foaming. Add the pears, flesh-side down, and cook for 2 to 3 minutes or until the pork is golden brown and crisp. Flip the pears and continue cooking for 2 to 3 minutes or until the other side is golden brown and crisp and the fruit is slightly soft.

Arrange the pears on a platter, sprinkle with flaky salt and crushed peppercorns, drizzle with honey, and serve immediately while still warm.

Potato Dumplings

RASPEBALLER

Today's potato dumplings evolved from flour-based dumplings. In fact, it wasn't until the eighteen hundreds, when the potato entered Norwegian society as a cheaper alternative to flour, that dumplings went from flour-based to potato-based.

I use my mother-in-law's dumpling recipe, but there are many variations served across the country. Some come with sausage and boiled meat, while others have meat stuffed inside. Some dumplings are topped with butter or fried bacon; some are served with a sauce made of brown cheese. There are also sweet versions drizzled with syrup or topped with lingonberries and sugar. They're all classic comfort food—a bit heavy but also fortifying.

Dumpling dough is sticky, so as you're forming it into balls, it can be helpful to wear plastic gloves and occasionally dip the spoon in a bowl of warm water. Avoid adding more flour, as the dough will get stiff and heavy and I find looser dough makes for tastier dumplings. • *serves 6*

FOR THE STOCK

About 2¼ pounds (1 kg) lightly salted lamb or pork knuckle

FOR THE DUMPLINGS

3⅓ pounds (1.5 kg) starchy potatoes, such as Beate, Kerr's Pink, or russet, peeled

1½ tablespoons all-purpose flour

2 cups (240 g) barley flour

½ tablespoon salt

½ teaspoon white pepper

For the stock, soak the salted lamb or pork in cold water for 24 hours then drain. Place the meat in a large, heavy pot and cover with fresh water. Bring to a boil then lower the heat to medium-low and gently simmer for 3 hours or until the meat is tender. Remove the meat and keep warm to make the dumplings. Reserve 2 quarts (2 l) of the stock to use for boiling the potato dumplings. Alternatively, you can use a stock of your choice, but make sure it has enough sodium to provide flavor for the dumplings.

If you have a meat grinder, cut the potatoes into 4 pieces and run through the grinder. Alternatively, grate the potatoes whole on the finest side of a box grater. If a lot of starchy liquid is released from the potatoes, pour it out and reserve for later use. In a large bowl, stir together the grated potatoes, all-purpose and barley flours, salt, and pepper. The dough should be somewhat wet but firm enough that it can be loosely shaped. If it's too stiff, gradually add some of the reserved potato water.

In a large, heavy pot, bring the reserved 2 quarts (2 l) stock to a gentle simmer, but don't let it boil.

Using a large metal spoon, form the dough into large balls that fit in the palm of your hand. Carefully drop the dumplings in the simmering stock and cook, stirring occasionally, for 30 minutes or until cooked through. Transfer the dumplings to a platter and serve with the reserved meat, sausages, boiled carrots, and boiled rutabaga. You can also garnish with fried bacon if desired.

Hen and Dumplings

HØNSESUPPE MED MELBOLLER

———————

Dumplings made of flour (*melboller*), often served in soup or cooked with milk, have been part of the Norwegian diet for some time. Hen soup with flour dumplings, most likely introduced from Denmark, was noted as far back as the seventeenth century. Despite chickens being found extensively across Norway, they were used mainly for egg production and it wasn't until much later that chickens became a staple of the diet.

For soup with dumplings, I prefer to use stewing hens, which no longer produce eggs. Their size and age yield a richer, more flavorful stock than commercial chickens, which are bred for their meat. Stewing hens require a bit more work and patience due to their tough meat, but the payoff is incredible, as they produce full-bodied stock with superior taste and texture. • *serves 6*

FOR THE SOUP

1 large stewing hen

2 large onions, quartered

2 large carrots, washed and roughly chopped

3 to 4 celery sticks with leaves, roughly chopped

6 cloves garlic, peeled

2 to 3 bay leaves

A few sprigs fresh thyme and flat-leaf parsley, plus chopped parsley for garnish

Salt and pepper

¼ cup (60 ml) heavy cream

FOR THE DUMPLINGS

1¼ cups (150 g) all-purpose flour, sifted

½ teaspoon ground cardamom

½ teaspoon granulated sugar

½ teaspoon salt

1 large egg, at room temperature

½ cup (120 ml) milk

4 tablespoons butter (56 g), melted

For the soup, in a large, heavy pot, combine the hen, onions, carrots, celery, celery leaves, garlic, bay leaves, thyme, and parsley. Season liberally with salt and pepper. Add enough cold water to cover the hen and bring to a boil. Lower the heat and gently simmer for at least 3 hours or until the meat is falling from the bones. Remove the pot from the heat and set aside to cool slightly. Strain the hen and vegetables from the stock. Discard the vegetables, but reserve the hen and set aside to cool. Return the stock to the pot and bring to a simmer. When the hen is cool, pull all the meat from the bones and shred it into large pieces; discard the carcass. Add the meat to the stock, followed by the heavy cream and season to taste with salt and pepper. Keep warm.

For the dumplings, in a large bowl, combine the flour, cardamom, sugar, and salt.

In a small bowl, whisk together the egg and milk. Add to the flour mixture, followed by the melted butter, and whisk until blended. Let stand 10 minutes.

Return the soup to a gentle simmer and set up a bowl of hot water.

Dip a small spoon in the hot water then use it to scoop out some of the dough and drop each spoonful into the simmering soup. Repeat with the rest of the dough. Once all the dumplings are in the soup, cook for 10 minutes or until the dumplings rise.

Divide the soup among bowls, garnish with chopped parsley, and serve.

Flatbread Yellow Pea Soup Wrap

ERTESUPPE-WRAP

Ertesuppe is a traditional pea soup served with flatbread and made with many items that would have been stored in a stabbur. It typically consists of dried yellow peas, vegetables, and a ham hock, pork knuckle, or cured sheep leg (fenalår). Sometimes barley and potatoes are added.

I came across an interesting tradition in southern Norway, where flatbread is dipped in water so it becomes soft again and then used as a type of wrap, with fish and other things folded inside. Inspired by this, I created a wrap using "resurrected" flatbread, and filled it with the tastes of traditional pea soup. If you don't have any flatbread on hand, use a whole-grain tortilla. For a vegetarian option, swap the meat for roasted potatoes. To save time, use quick-cooking barley. • _serves 4_

FOR THE YELLOW PEA PURÉE

1 tablespoon lightly salted butter

1 onion, diced

1 cup dried yellow peas, soaked overnight and drained

3 cups (720 ml) water

¾ teaspoon salt, divided

1 clove garlic

1 tablespoon freshly squeezed lemon juice

FOR THE WRAPS

2 carrots, peeled and cut into very thin matchsticks

1 tablespoon freshly squeezed lemon juice

2 large or 4 small flatbreads (page 149)

1½ cups (265 g) cooked barley

2½ ounces (70 g) baby arugula or spinach

1 small rutabaga, peeled and cut into very thin matchsticks

1 leek, washed and thinly sliced

Chopped fresh chives

About 3 pounds (1.4 kg) meat from a cooked ham hock or cured leg of lamb

Pepper

For the yellow pea purée, in a medium, heavy saucepan, melt the butter over medium-high heat. Add the onion and sauté for 5 minutes or until soft and translucent. Add the dried yellow peas, water, and ¼ teaspoon salt, lower the heat, and gently simmer for about 1½ hours or until the peas are soft. Remove from the heat and let cool slightly. In a food processor, combine the pea purée with the garlic, lemon juice, and the remaining ½ teaspoon salt and process until smooth. Set aside.

For the wraps, in a small bowl, toss the julienned carrots with the lemon juice and let stand for about 20 minutes.

Prepare the flatbreads by fully immersing them in lukewarm water. Remove the flatbreads from the water and wrap each one in a clean towel for 2 to 3 minutes or until soft. If using large flatbreads, cut them in half to make 4 servings.

Generously smear the pea purée on each flatbread and top with carrots, barley, arugula, rutabaga, leeks, and chives. Arrange a good portion of meat on each flatbread and season to taste with pepper. To roll the wraps, fold the sides in first, then roll up the bottom a third of the way up. Tuck it under and continue rolling upwards. Cut each wrap in half and serve.

Bålet

THE CAMPFIRE

The campfire is synonymous with warmth and light; its flames flickering upwards in a mesmerizing dance. It's primitive and yet sophisticated, and has a multifold purpose. A controlled, open fire elevates the experience of any meal, from the way you prepare the food—a task that often requires patience, as the ingredients cook slowly over the flames—to the flavors and textures of the finished dish.

In Norway, the season for outdoor fires typically runs between September and April, when temperatures are cooler and there's less risk of fires spreading. Around this time, there's very little to deter one from being outdoors, especially when you have a Norwegian mindset. Here, you will always be reminded of the saying, "There is no such thing as bad weather, only bad clothing." This attitude means you can enjoy the outdoors no matter if there's rain, wind, snow, or sunshine. All you need is a little preparedness and a positive attitude.

The deep connection and attitude Norwegians have toward nature means a lot of meals are prepared outdoors and over an open fire. It's more than campfire cooking, but rather a way of being. In this, the concept of *bålkos* is born, which is the atmosphere created by and around the fire, and what sets the tone and mood of the experience.

An intuitive sense of bålkos seems to run through the DNA of most, if not all, Norwegians. With this mindset, a rugged landscape is turned into a comfortable and idyllic setting almost instantaneously. Makeshift sitting areas are created with delicate moss, dry planks and twigs, and even warm, furry sheepskins on chilly days. The coffee pot, blackened from many uses, is hung over the fire. Cups are filled and passed around so everyone can partake. It's not uncommon to see the little ones drinking watered down fruit cordial or decadent hot chocolate. The meal is unpacked and smooth rocks and tree stumps become improvised tables. Sticks are whittled into utensils and loosened tree bark is used for plates. Nature evolves into a dynamic kitchen and everything centers around the fire. But, bålkos is more than just the physical setting; it's also the mood and the interactions around the fire. It's the meal itself.

Typical campfire food, referred to as *bålmat,* includes both quick and slow-cooked meals. It's typical for sausages, waffles, stick breads, pancakes, seared fish, stews, meats, and hot drinks to make an appearance. The ingredients can be prepared ahead and brought along in packed containers and thermoses, or gathered right then from nature. A day of fishing or hunting might provide the main course. Foraging might yield wild berries, mushrooms, and herbs. Sometimes a meal can be unplanned—a spontaneous dining experience amidst the wild surroundings.

Cooking over a fire can be done in a variety of ways. Food can be placed directly on the embers or coals, over a grill that's hung from above, placed on top of a stone slab, or even held over the fire with sticks. I find cooking on embers and coals to be incredibly enjoyable, with a little ash easily brushed off. The setting can be in the middle of nature, in the yard, or in specialty cabins built for grilling. Whatever the location, please take caution when cooking with fire and never leave it unattended. Being responsible ensures an unforgettable experience, one that's focused on the conversations, the stillness, the natural surroundings, and the stirring of the fire.

In this chapter, I share popular meals cooked over the fire, ones sure to please adults and kids alike. I include different methods of cooking, be it a leg of lamb hung over the fire or trout attached to wooden planks and set nearby. Many of the recipes from the other chapters can also be carried over as campfire meals. The idea is to enjoy the time spent outdoors and to make the most of simple, fresh ingredients. Cooking delicious meals over the fire doesn't have to require massive amounts of work and cleanup. In fact, it can often be the opposite. An incredible dining experience in nature is only part of what makes bålkos; the rest is in the atmosphere, simplicity, and tranquility, as well as in drawing meaning from each and every moment.

Ember Grilled Leeks
with Butter

GRILLET PURRE MED SMØR

───────────

Cooking vegetables directly on glowing embers enhances their flavor and minimizes cleanup. Leeks are ideal for this approach, because their outer layers act as a barrier, allowing the leeks to steam from the inside. Those outer layers, which are burnt and covered in ash, can then be easily peeled away to reveal soft, sweet flesh. Topped with butter and sea salt, these leeks make an excellent side dish. I imagine smoked salt or herb-infused butter would taste great on these as well. *serves 4*

4 large or 8 small leeks   Flaky salt
Unsalted butter

Prepare a fire and allow it to burn down so you have glowing embers to cook on. Place the leeks directly on top of the embers and cook, turning a few times, for 15 to 20 minutes or until the outside layers are charred. Trim the ends off the leeks and peel off the charred layers. Cut lengthwise and immediately spread with a good amount of butter, letting it melt over the leeks. Sprinkle with flaky salt and serve.

Twisted Bread with Carrots and Oats

PINNEBRØD

Pinnebrød, which means, "stick bread," is one of the more common campfire foods in Norway. It's a favorite, especially among kids. Sticks are gathered and each person pulls off a piece of dough to wrap around the top of their stick and turn slowly over the open flame. The dough puffs up beautifully and forms a lightly burnished crust.

I've added some whole-wheat flour, oats, and carrots to the traditional recipe for a more hearty and flavorful bread. The coarse texture requires a little more help when being wrapped around the stick, so be sure to press the ends together. Feel free to eat the bread as is, or cook it wrapped around sausage for a more complete meal. · *serves 6 to 8*

1¼ cups (150 g) whole-wheat flour

1¼ cups (150 g) all-purpose flour, sifted

½ cup (50 g) quick-cooking oats

1 tablespoon baking powder

½ teaspoon salt

¾ cup (180 ml) milk

¼ cup (60 ml) mild-flavored oil

2 tablespoons runny honey

2 carrots, peeled and finely grated

Crushed walnuts (optional)

Sticks for cooking

In a large bowl, combine the whole-wheat and all-purpose flours, oats, baking powder, and salt. Add the milk, oil, honey, carrots, and walnuts, if using, and stir with a wooden spoon to combine.

Gather enough sticks (1 per person) and use a sharp knife to remove the top layers of bark. Take a small handful of dough and form it into a roughly ½-inch-thick (1.25 cm) snake shape. Wrap the dough around the top of the stick, leaving enough room at the bottom to safely hold the stick near the fire. Repeat with the remaining dough.

Hold the sticks over the embers rather than directly over the flames—the flames can quickly burn the crust, but leave the inside doughy. Cook for 10 minutes or until the dough is cooked through. Carefully remove the bread from the sticks and cool slightly before diving in.

Stone Slab Fish and Potatoes

FISK PÅ STEINHELLE

————————

This is a very primitive way to cook fresh fish. In fact, cooking over stone is the first known method of cooking with fire. You don't need any pots or pans, just a dry stone slab—slate is ideal—and a fire. The taste you get from cooking on stone is incredible and you can toss on a variety of vegetables and wild herbs, as well as warm some bread, to make a complete meal out of it. It's very important that the slate slab is completely dry; otherwise, it can crack and burst during the cooking process. • *serves 4*

8 new potatoes

1 dry slate slab

Lightly salted butter, for cooking

4 shallots, peeled and cut lengthwise in half

Additional vegetables (optional)

1 fresh trout or other freshwater fish, cleaned and gutted

Salt and pepper

A few sprigs fresh thyme

In a medium pot, cover the potatoes with cold salted water and bring to a boil. Lower the heat and simmer for 10 to 15 minutes, until the potatoes are barely tender when pierced with a knife. Drain the potatoes and set aside.

Prepare a small fire with logs, making sure you have extra logs on hand to feed the fire as the slate slab heats up. Place large stones next to the fire and arrange the slab so it balances on the stones and is about 2 inches (5 cm) above the glowing embers. After 20 minutes, check if the stone is hot enough by adding a small dab of butter; when it quickly melts and foams, the slab is ready.

Place a good amount of butter on the stone. Cut the potatoes lengthwise in half. Arrange the potatoes and shallots, along with additional vegetables, if using, around the edges of the slab and cook, turning occasionally, for 5 to 10 minutes or until golden.

Sprinkle the trout, inside and out, with salt and pepper and put a couple thyme sprigs inside. Place the fish in the center of the stone, surrounded by the potatoes and shallots. Toss a few more thyme sprigs on top and cook, turning once, until the flesh is opaque and easily falling from the bone. Serve the fish warm, with the cooked potatoes and shallots.

Slow-Roasted Leg of Lamb with Dill and Orange Sauce

LANGTIDSSTEKT LAMMELÅR MED DILL- OG APPELSINSAUS

Lamb is available year-round, but the high times for eating it are during Easter (*Påske*) and in the autumn months, after the lambs have returned from grazing in the mountains. I always view leg of lamb as a feast dish, and think it's an ideal meal for friends and family to gather around the fire and slow down for a couple of hours. I like to serve lamb with a dill and orange sauce that's inspired by the incredible amount of oranges Norwegians consume throughout the Easter holiday. *serves 10 to 12*

FOR THE DILL AND ORANGE SAUCE

Zest of 1 orange plus ¼ cup (60 ml) freshly squeezed orange juice

2 tablespoons freshly squeezed lemon juice

3 cloves garlic, minced

¾ teaspoon salt

¼ cup (60 ml) fresh dill, coarsely chopped

1 cup (240 ml) fresh flat-leaf parsley, coarsely chopped

½ cup (120 ml) olive oil

FOR THE LAMB

1 (6¾-pound / 3-kg) bone-in leg of lamb

Mild-flavored oil

4 cloves garlic, minced

Salt and pepper

About 1 hour before starting to cook the lamb, prepare a fire to get a nice core of glowing embers. Continue feeding the fire as needed throughout the cooking process.

Let the lamb stand at room temperature for 1 hour before cooking.

For the dill and orange sauce, in a small serving bowl, whisk together the orange and lemon juice, garlic, and salt. Add the dill, parsley, and orange zest. Slowly drizzle in the olive oil, whisking until emulsified. Let stand for at least 1 hour to infuse; whisk before serving.

For the lamb, rub some oil and the garlic over the lamb. Season to taste with salt and pepper. Place a metal hook through the anklebone and tie a good knot around the hook with heavy twine or wire. Hang the lamb over the prepared fire, suspended from a campfire tripod or other device and 1½ to 3 feet (45 to 90 cm) away from the coals. Cook, occasionally lowering, lifting, and turning the lamb to ensure even cooking, for 3 to 4 hours or until the meat reaches an internal temperature of 135°F (57°C). The lamb will be more well done near the thigh and more rare toward the ankle. Let the lamb rest for 10 to 15 minutes before carving. Drizzle the dill and orange sauce over the lamb or serve it alongside.

Nordic-Inspired Hot Dogs

PØLSER

Norwegians love their sausage, especially cooked over a fire. The most "Norwegian" way to serve sausage is wrapped in *lompe*, which are soft potato flatbreads, and topped with ketchup, mustard, and crispy onions. While this is very delicious, I wanted to elevate the typical sausage and play on some iconic ingredients like strawberries, sweet and sour cabbage, lingonberry jam, and beer. So, here are my five Nordic-inspired topping suggestions to take any sausage experience to the next level. See the next page for my favorite combinations of these toppings. • *serves 6 to 8*

FOR THE AIOLI BASE

2 large egg yolks, at room temperature

2 cloves garlic, minced

1 tablespoon freshly squeezed lemon juice

1 teaspoon Dijon mustard

1 cup (240 ml) mild-flavored oil

Salt and pepper to taste

To make dill aioli, add:
1½ tablespoons chopped fresh dill

To make horseradish aioli, add:
3 tablespoons freshly grated horseradish

To make dark ale aioli, add:
⅓ cup (80 ml) dark ale

FOR THE STRAWBERRY KETCHUP

2 tablespoons mild-flavored oil

1 red onion, diced

2 whole cloves

¼ teaspoon ground coriander

¼ teaspoon ground cinnamon

9 ounces (250 g) vine tomatoes, roughly chopped

9 ounces (250 g) strawberries, hulled and roughly chopped

¼ cup (60 ml) distilled white vinegar, divided

1 tablespoon dark brown sugar

Salt and pepper

FOR THE CRISPY ONIONS

2 tablespoons mild-flavored oil

2 large yellow onions, cut into thin rings

⅛ teaspoon salt

FOR THE PEA RELISH

1 cup frozen peas, thawed

½ yellow onion, finely diced

Zest of 1 lemon

Salt and pepper

FOR THE CRISPY MUSHROOMS

1 tablespoon lightly salted butter

3 tablespoons mild-flavored oil

9 ounces (250 g) button mushrooms, trimmed and cut into small pieces

FOR THE NO-DRESSING SLAW

1 cup finely chopped red cabbage

1 cup finely chopped fennel

FOR SERVING

Sausages, hot dog buns, sharp cheese, blue cheese crumbles, bacon, sliced pickled beets, sweet and sour red cabbage (*rødkål*) (page 101), strong mustard, cream cheese (preferably made with goat's milk), lingonberry jam, diced apples

For the aioli, in a medium bowl, combine the egg yolks, garlic, lemon juice, and mustard. Slowly drizzle in the oil, whisking until thick. Stir in the dill, horseradish, or dark ale, depending on which aioli you're making; season to taste with salt and pepper.

For the strawberry ketchup, in a large, heavy pot, heat the oil over medium-high heat. Add the red onion, cloves, coriander, and cinnamon and sauté for 5 minutes or until the onion is soft and translucent. Add the tomatoes, strawberries, 2 tablespoons (30 ml) of the vinegar, and the brown sugar and simmer for 30 minutes. Transfer to a food processor or blender and pulse until smooth. Add the remaining 2 tablespoons (30 ml) vinegar and season to taste with salt and pepper.

For the crispy onions, in a large, heavy pan, heat the oil over medium-high heat. Add the yellow onions, lower to medium heat, season with the salt, and sauté for about 20 minutes or until darker in color and a little crispy. Keep warm.

For the pea relish, in a small bowl, combine the peas, yellow onion, and lemon zest. Season to taste with salt and pepper.

For the crispy mushrooms, in a large, heavy pan, heat the butter and oil over medium-high heat. Add the mushrooms and sauté for 20 to 30 minutes or until they crisp up and lose their moisture.

For the no-dressing slaw, in a medium bowl, toss together the cabbage and fennel.

Here are five of my favorite hot dog combinations:

THE SUMMER DOG: **Strawberry ketchup, dill aioli, and no-dressing slaw**
Slather one side of the bun with strawberry ketchup and the other with dill aioli. Add the cooked sausage and top with slaw.

THE VIKING: **Sharp cheese, dark ale aioli, and crispy onions**
Melt sharp cheese of your choice and place inside the bun. Add the cooked sausage, dark ale aioli, and caramelized, crispy onions.

THE UNDERDOG: **Bacon-wrapped sausage, horseradish aioli, pickled beets, and blue cheese crumbles**
Wrap the entire uncooked sausage with 1 to 2 pieces of uncooked bacon. Grill until the sausage is cooked through and the bacon is crispy. Place the sausage in the bun and top with horseradish aioli, pickled beets, and blue cheese crumbles.

THE MOUNTAIN FARM: **Pea relish, crispy mushrooms, and lingonberry jam**
Place the cooked sausage in the bun. Add pea relish on one side and lingonberry jam on the other. Top with crispy mushrooms.

THE ZINGER: **Sweet and sour red cabbage (rødkål), strong mustard, and cream cheese (optional: diced apples)**
Spread cream cheese on the bun. Add the cooked sausage and top with strong mustard, sweet and sour red cabbage, and diced apples, if using.

Wood Plank Trout

PLANKEFISK

Edged against the river in Numedal lies the Medieval Forest, an emerging area dedicated to the preservation of history, culture, and traditional skills. It was here that I first learned about the eating habits during the medieval and Viking ages from Kjell and Maj-Lis, the passionate husband and wife team central to the preservation of medieval culture in this valley. They taught me just how simple it is to cook fish on wood planks.

As the fish sits upright next to the open flame, it slowly cooks, with its juices dripping down and its skin crisping. The aroma is captivating and it's easy to fall into a trance, while you stare into the glowing flames surrounded by the wildness of nature. It's hands-on cooking, with a bit of theatrics, but it makes the whole experience even more special. This recipe uses shallots and fresh herbs, which were known to be used by the Vikings; the lemon may or may not be quite as authentic. If ground elder is not accessible, substitute it with fresh parsley. • *serves 4 to 6*

2 wood planks (see below)	1 bunch fresh thyme, roughly chopped
Sticks for cooking	1 bunch ground elder, roughly chopped
1 whole trout	1 lemon, thinly sliced
2 shallots, thinly sliced	Salt

To cook 1 whole trout, you'll need 2 wood planks. Each plank should be 1-inch thick (2.5 cm) and measure about 8 x 20 inches (20 x 50 cm), depending on the size of the fish. Toward the middle of each plank, carve four small holes, the thickness of a little finger, for the wood pegs to hold the fish. The holes should be measured against the fish, with 2 holes across from each other, about 2 inches (5 cm) below the top of the fish, and 2 holes across from each other, about 3 inches (7.5 cm) above the bottom of the fish.

Prepare 8 wood pegs by removing the bark from 8 sticks and whittling them down. The pegs need to fit inside the holes in the wood planks, so the bottom of each should be slightly thinner than the thickness of a little finger. Set the planks and pegs aside while you prepare the fish.

Remove the head and insides of the fish then clean and rinse it. Slice the fish lengthwise in half, leaving the skin on. Spread the shallots, thyme, and elder evenly over the flesh side of each fillet. Arrange lemon slices on top and season to taste with salt. Carefully flip each fillet, flesh-side down, onto a wood plank. Using 4 pegs per fillet, attach the fish to the plank, carefully hammering the pegs into the plank with the back of a knife, as needed. Place the planks upright next to the fire, using large stones for support. Cook for about 30 minutes then flip the planks vertically to ensure even cooking. Continue cooking for about 30 minutes or until the flesh is bright and pulls off easily. Serve warm.

Homemade Blueberry Marshmallows

HJEMMELAGDE BLÅBÆRMARSHMALLOWS

————————

I'm a big fan of homemade marshmallows, especially those flavored with fresh berries. They have an incredible taste and the texture is so smooth and spongy. I usually use European blueberries, which are called bilberries, because they're so plentiful and grow wild everywhere around us. Plus, they give the marshmallows a gorgeous color. Of course, any type of blueberry will work.

Bring these along to your next campfire and toss one or two in a cup of hot chocolate, or eat them straight from the tin. They don't hold up very well when roasted over the fire, but a few seconds should be enough for a gooey treat. · *makes about 30*

½ cup (60 g) cornstarch

½ cup (50 g) confectioners' sugar

10 ounces (280 g) frozen blueberries

1½ cups (300 g) granulated sugar

½ cup (120 ml) water

¼ cup (60 ml) runny honey

10 (3 x 4½-inch / 7.5 x 11.5-cm) gelatin sheets or ¾ ounce (21 g) gelatin powder

1 teaspoon vanilla extract

Oil a 9 x 13-inch (22.5 x 32.5 cm) baking pan. Line the pan with parchment paper and oil the parchment.

In a small bowl, combine the cornstarch and confectioners' sugar. Sprinkle some on the bottom of the prepared pan. Reserve the remaining cornstarch mixture.

In a medium saucepan, bring the frozen blueberries to a boil. Lower the heat and simmer, pressing the berries to release their juices, for 5 minutes or until the berries break down. Press the fruit through a mesh strainer into a small bowl. Measure ½ cup (120 ml) and keep warm; reserve any extra for another use.

In a medium, heavy pot, combine the granulated sugar, water, and honey over medium heat to dissolve the sugar. Raise the heat and bring to a simmer. Continue cooking, without stirring, for about 12 minutes or until the mixture registers 240°F (116°C) on a candy thermometer.

Meanwhile, soak the gelatin sheets in about 2 cups (480 ml) cold water for 5 minutes. Squeeze the water from the gelatin sheets, add them to the reserved ½ cup (120 ml) warm blueberry purée, and stir until completely dissolved. (If using gelatin powder, sprinkle it directly into the warm blueberry purée.) Pour the purée into the bowl of a stand mixer fitted with the whisk attachment.

When the sugar mixture has reached 240°F (116°C), immediately add it to the blueberry purée in the stand mixer—it's very hot and will bubble up so take caution. Add the vanilla extract. Whisk on low for 1 minute then increase the speed to medium-high and whisk for up to 10 minutes or until the mixture is stiff but spreadable. Pour into the prepared pan, dust with the reserved cornstarch mixture, and let stand, uncovered, for about 3 hours or until firm.

Lift the marshmallows out of the pan using the parchment paper and cut into large squares. Store in an airtight container at room temperature for up to 2 weeks.

Fire-Brewed Coffee

BÅLKAFFE

Though it dates back as far as the sixteen hundreds, coffee wasn't common in Norway until the nineteenth century. It was originally sold as raw, green beans, and roasted at home. This was because roasted coffee loses its flavor after some time and before the nineteen hundreds and modern transportation, it couldn't be distributed fast enough.

Today, Norwegians import close to ten kilos per person of coffee each year, which is just below Finland, and makes Norway the second largest consumer in the world. It's been calculated that Norwegians drink up to 5 cups of coffee a day. Perhaps it's the cold weather or maybe it's the quality of the beans and the water they're brewed in. Whatever the case, coffee is the unofficial drink of Norway, and one of the best ways to serve it, I believe, is over an open fire. What makes fire-brewed coffee so special is the authenticity and method, not to mention the incredible atmosphere. You would be hard pressed to find a Norwegian campfire without any coffee. While coffee is typically served without milk and sugar, you are more than welcome to bring some along.

serves 4

4¼ cups (1 l) water

10 tablespoons or 2 ounces (56 g) of coarsely ground coffee

In an outdoor coffee pot, bring the water to a boil over an open fire. Carefully remove the pot from the fire, stir in the coffee, and let steep, with the lid on, for 5 minutes before serving. If some of the grounds are on top, just do a quick stir to let them settle to the bottom before serving.

Pass cups of coffee around the campfire and enjoy.

Cardamom Hot Chocolate

VARM SJOKOLADE MED KARDEMOMME

Hot chocolate is synonymous with the Norwegian concept of *kos* or *hygge,* which is a feeling of coziness. It conjures images of knitted mittens grasping ceramic cups with steam filtering upwards and kettles hanging over open fires in the vast Norwegian landscape. It also makes me think of heading indoors, following a day of skiing, to enjoy the mountain cabin, where there are blankets, wool socks, a fireplace blazing, and the smell of cocoa in the air.

When we're having hot chocolate by the fire, someone usually brings along a few sweet buns (*boller*) to share. The buns, in typical Norwegian fashion, have a subtle hint of cardamom in every bite. Dipping them into the cocoa is an accepted practice that I'm always more than happy to indulge in. It was this cardamom and chocolate infusion that inspired me to bring them together in one sultry cup of cocoa. The result is a creamy, subtly rich drink that will satisfy all on its own, but a sweet bun or two served alongside wouldn't hurt either. • *makes 4 servings*

4 cups (960 ml) whole milk

16 green cardamom pods, gently crushed

2 ounces (56 g) good-quality dark chocolate, chopped

2 teaspoons vanilla extract

Whipped cream, shaved chocolate, and ground cardamom, for serving

In a medium, heavy saucepan, slowly heat the milk and cardamom over medium heat, whisking occasionally, for 10 to 15 minutes or until the milk reaches its boiling point. Remove from the heat and scoop out the cardamom pods. Add the chopped chocolate and vanilla extract and whisk until the chocolate is melted. Divide the hot chocolate among mugs and top with whipped cream, shaved chocolate, and ground cardamom. Serve immediately.

Jernet, Takken, og Ovnen

THE IRON, THE GRIDDLE, AND THE OVEN

The iron, the griddle, and the oven have each played a vital role in shaping the baking culture in Norway. They've been used to make food out of necessity, as well as for pleasure, and as they've evolved over time, they've changed the way we bake both inside and outside the home.

One of the most delightful and simple pleasures in life is the smell of dough and batter cooking. Whether it's from a waffle in a waffle iron, thick cakes on top of a griddle, or even bread in the oven, there's a comfort in the aromas and warmth that exude from baked goods. It's something most of us can relate to and it often connects us to some of our fondest memories.

Baking has evolved from its humble beginnings when the ingredients were simple and the cooking methods primitive. It's fascinating to look back over the centuries to see how baking's evolution affected the Norwegian diet and which dishes continue to be widely eaten today.

During the Viking era, women were responsible for overseeing the grains and keeping them free from mold. They ground the flour by hand in small batches to be used within a few days before the flour could go bad. They made *brødtallerken,* a soft bread consisting of flour, salt, and water that was cooked on a round (roughly 10 ½-inch / 27-cm) pan with a long handle. The bread was laid out on the middle of the table, and topped with fish or meat. It's sometimes compared to Italian pizza, without a leavening agent in the dough.

When water mills began being built around local streams in the thirteen hundreds, men took over milling the grains. Milling could only be done when the water levels were high, which meant mills produced large quantities of flour at a time. It was difficult to use the flour before it spoiled, so the women developed a new approach and began baking hard flatbreads (*flatbrød*), which could be stored for longer periods of time and stacked on top of one another. To create these new breads, the women needed the right cooking equipment, which led to the creation of the *takke,* a large, flat griddle.

Some women folded the new flatbreads over, as a replacement for the brød-tallerken, while others soaked them in water to soften them before serving. These softened flatbreads became known as *lefse,* which is still one of the most internationally recognized breads of Norway. When grain imports from Denmark were blockaded during the Napoleonic Wars, flour was rationed and potatoes became more widely used. Women began mixing small amounts of flour with mashed, cooked potatoes to make soft flatbreads called *potetlefse. Lompe*, a smaller variety of lefse, made with a lot of potatoes and relatively little flour, was developed for the same reason.

In the sixteen hundreds, iron started to be used more often for baking flat cakes, such as *goro*, and textured cakes like waffles. Initially, the irons were heavy with long handles for holding over an open fire, but when cast-iron wood-burning stoves became more common, the long-handled iron was replaced with one that could rest on top of the stove.

The introduction of household stoves, which didn't happen until the late eighteen hundreds, had an even more significant impact on baking culture, and created almost endless opportunities for home cooking and baking. Previously, baking was done in open fire pits or in professional bakers' ovens, which could only be found in towns or monasteries. Being a baker by profession developed quite early in Norway, especially in the city of Bergen. In fact, when German bakers arrived in Bergen in the thirteen hundreds, they established Norway's very first baker's guild.

When the twentieth century brought electricity to Norway, it was deemed a "modern miracle." Electricity paved the way for the electric stove, and also meant that other household appliances, such as the waffle iron and takke, were converted to electric.

Baking is now easier and more accessible, but older methods and appliances still have their place in the kitchen. For instance, I have older irons for waffles and wafer cookies (*krumkaker*) that I always use when camping, and some women in my area continue to bake lefse and flatbreads on top of their wood-burning stoves, which gives those baked goods unique flavor and texture.

The recipes in this chapter are baked in an iron, on top of a griddle, or in the oven. Norwegian waffle irons, *krumkake* irons, munk pans, and griddles can all be purchased from specialty shops or online. You can also substitute a regular frying pan or cast-iron skillet for the Norwegian griddle, as I have tested the recipes on both. At the end of the day, baking is as much a necessity as a reflection of the love and care put into each baked good.

Aniseed Waffles

ANISVAFLER

Norwegian waffles bring new meaning to the expression, "Home is where the heart is." These delightful, heart-shaped treats embrace the very essence of the Norwegian feeling of coziness called *kos* or *hygge.* Waffles can be cooked outside, over an open fire, or in the warmth of a kitchen. A long hike, a day spent skiing in the mountains, celebrations with friends and family, and even long, quiet afternoons are all reasons to bring out the waffle iron. The sweet aroma whiffing through the air always summons a feeling of elation.

Vafler derives from the German *wafel,* which means "honeycomb." The pattern of the iron plates originated in the thirteenth century, and is modelled after beeswax cakes from the hive. It's no wonder the waffles we know today originate from something as sweet as honey.

During the seventeenth and eighteenth centuries, waffle irons featured a long handle plus a cast-iron plate that was either rectangular or in the shape of a single heart. It wasn't until much later that the iron changed to five hearts inside a circle, the shape that's now so closely associated with Scandinavia.

I took a little creative license with my waffle recipe, and swapped cardamom for anise, another spice that reminds me of Norway. Its delicate taste is reminiscent of licorice yet softer and sweeter. It complements the texture of the waffles and adds a bit of freshness with each bite. All these waffles need is a dollop of whipped cream or a dusting of confectioners' sugar, but jam, sour cream, and other toppings are delicious as well. · *makes 10 waffles*

3 large eggs, at room temperature

½ cup (100 g) granulated sugar

¾ cup plus 1 tablespoon (200 ml) milk

¾ cup plus 1 tablespoon (200 ml) buttermilk

½ cup plus 1 tablespoon (125 g) lightly salted butter, melted

1¾ cups (210 g) all-purpose flour, sifted

1 teaspoon baking soda

2½ teaspoons aniseed, finely crushed

In a large bowl, combine the eggs and granulated sugar and whisk until fluffy. Add the milk, buttermilk, and melted butter.

In a medium bowl, whisk together the flour, baking soda, and crushed aniseed. Add to the egg mixture and gently whisk to combine, making sure there are no lumps. Let stand for 15 to 20 minutes.

Heat and butter a waffle iron. Spoon some of the batter onto the iron, close, and bake for 3 to 5 minutes or until the waffle has the desired texture. Repeat with the remaining batter.

Serve warm with whipped cream, confectioners' sugar, jam, or sour cream.

Pancake Puffs

MUNKER

Munker are traditional spherical pancakes that somewhat resemble doughnuts. They're cooked in a distinctive cast-iron pan called a *munkejern* and though they have deep roots in southern Norway, especially the city of Arendal, they originate from Denmark, where they're called *æbleskiver* (apple slices).

Munker is a curious term and may—big emphasis on *may*—be more closely connected to the Dutch version of æbleskiver, which are called *poffertjes.* According to one legend, when monks faced a flour shortage during the French Revolution, they used buckwheat to make self-rising pancakes to be used as holy bread and the recipe was so good, it spread throughout the villages. A blacksmith was ordered to make a furnace with hundreds of shallow holes on the top plate and they began calling the cakes by a name that translates to "little friars." The noise made by air escaping when the pancakes were finished cooking and puffing up led to their current name, poffertjes.

It's possible the original name was carried across to Norway, and translated to the Norwegian word for monks, especially since the Dutch have had such a large impact on the food culture of southern Norway. Whatever the real story is, these pancakes are incredibly tasty and quite fun to make. All you need is a little patience and a munk/æbleskiver pan. · *makes about 30*

1¼ cups (250 g) granulated sugar

3 large eggs, at room temperature

1 cup plus 2 teaspoons (250 ml) whole milk

4 cups plus 2 tablespoons (500 g) all-purpose flour, sifted

2½ teaspoons baking soda

About ½ cup (112 g) lightly salted butter, melted, for frying

Confectioners' sugar, for serving

In a large bowl, combine the granulated sugar and eggs and whisk until creamy. Add the milk, followed by the flour and baking soda, whisking to make sure there are no lumps. Let stand for at least 30 minutes.

Place the munk pan directly on the stove over medium heat. Add a small spoonful of melted butter to each of the holes and when the butter foams, fill the holes two-thirds full with batter. Cook the munker until they begin to stiffen on the bottom. Continue cooking, frequently turning with a wooden skewer or fork and adding more butter as needed to prevent sticking, for 8 to 10 minutes or until the outsides are golden brown and a toothpick inserted in the center comes out clean. Repeat with the remaining batter, adding more butter and reheating the pan as needed.

Dust the munker with confectioners' sugar and serve warm—they're also lovely with jam and fruit compotes.

Norwegian Wafer Cookies with Juniper Berry and Espresso Creams

KRUMKAKER

————————

Krumkake is simply a sweetened, wafer-thin cookie rolled into a cone-shape, but it's one of the most classic and possibly oldest cookies eaten at Christmas. The batter is cooked in a special iron called a *krumkakejern*. It's embellished with an intricate design that brands the cookies with an elegant pattern that would fancify any table.

Cookies so thin and delicate that they shatter into tiny pieces when pressed are deemed the best and this recipe yields just such cookies. I was so grateful when my friend Lise was happy to share her grandmother's delicious recipe for this book.

I like to serve krumkake with espresso-infused whipped cream with a pronounced coffee flavor, as well as juniper berry-infused whipped cream that's earthier and more subtle. Plan to start this dish one day ahead so the creams have time to infuse. • *makes about 25*

FOR THE CREAMS
2 cups (480 ml) heavy cream, divided

½ cup (35 g) espresso beans

¼ cup (17 g) dried juniper berries, gently crushed

1½ teaspoons granulated sugar, divided

FOR THE COOKIES
½ cup plus 1 tablespoon (125 g) margarine, melted

1 cup (200 g) granulated sugar

1 large egg, separated, at room temperature

1 cup (120 g) all-purpose flour, sifted

1 cup (240 ml) lukewarm water

1 cup (120 g) potato starch

For the creams, combine 1 cup (240 ml) of the heavy cream with the espresso beans in a clean glass jar with a lid. In a second clean glass jar with a lid, combine the remaining 1 cup (240 ml) heavy cream with the juniper berries. Seal both jars and refrigerate overnight. Strain creams into separate bowls; discard the beans and juniper berries. Whip the espresso cream and 1 teaspoon sugar until stiff peaks form. Repeat with the juniper berry cream, but only add ½ teaspoon sugar.

For the cookies, in a large bowl, whisk together the melted margarine and sugar. Add the egg yolk, followed by some of the flour, some of the water, and some of the potato starch, whisking to combine. Continue alternating to add the remaining flour, water, and potato starch. Lightly beat the egg white and gently fold into the batter.

Place the krumkakejern directly on the stove over medium-high heat or follow the manufacturer's directions if using an electric iron. When the iron is hot, add a little butter at the start to prevent sticking. Depending on the desired thickness, spoon 1 to 2 tablespoons batter on the iron. Close the iron and cook, flipping once, for about 30 seconds per side, or until light golden. Carefully remove the cookie from the iron and immediately wrap it around a cone-shaped mold for 30 seconds or until firm. Transfer to a wire rack to cool and repeat with the remaining batter.

Serve the creams inside or alongside the cookies.

Potato Lefse from Tinn

TINN-LEFSER

There are so many variations of *lefse* that it's hard to pick just one, but I really adore this recipe. It was passed down to my friend Kari from her grandmother, who came from the area of Tinn in Telemark. Kari and her sister get together every year to make a large batch of lefse to last until the next baking session.

This type of lefse is rolled out thin and large, and can be wrapped around savory ingredients or layered with butter and sugar. Kari humbly gives most of the baking credit to her sister, but it's a joint effort that results in a soft flatbread that's both versatile and delicious. It's best to cook lefse on a cool day, as heat makes it harder to roll out the dough. Be sure to prep the potatoes a day before making the bread. • *makes 16*

2¼ pounds (1 kg) starchy potatoes, such as Beate, Kerr's Pink, or russet

1 cup plus 2 teaspoons (250 ml) whole milk

7½ to 8½ cups (900 g to 1 kg) all-purpose flour, sifted, plus more for rolling

½ cup (110 g) margarine, room temperature and crumbled into small pieces

¾ cup plus 1 tablespoon (200 ml) sour cream

3 tablespoons heavy cream

In a large pot, cover the potatoes with cold salted water and bring to a boil. Lower the heat and simmer for 20 minutes or until the potatoes are barely tender when pierced with a knife. Drain the potatoes and cool slightly. Peel the potatoes then run through a ricer twice. Cover and refrigerate overnight.

The next day, in a small saucepan, bring the milk to a simmer then let cool.

In the bowl of a stand mixer, combine the chilled potatoes with 7½ cups (900 g) of the flour. Add the heated and cooled milk, along with the margarine, sour cream, and heavy cream and blend until combined. If the dough is sticky, gradually add up to 1 cup (100 g) flour until the dough is workable.

Divide the dough into 16 equal portions (about 5 ounces / 140 g each) or into 32 portions (about 2½ ounces / 70 g each) if using a large nonstick frying pan. Shape each portion into a round.

On a well-floured surface, use a rolling pin and a circular motion from the center outward to roll out each round of dough into a very thin circle, about 18 inches (46 cm) in diameter if using a takke or 9 inches (23 cm) if using a pan; add more flour as needed to prevent sticking. The trick is to get the lefse as thin as possible without tearing. If the dough does tear, use your fingers to press it back together. Using a soft-bristled brush, brush off any excess flour.

Heat a takke to medium-high heat or place a large frying pan directly on the stove over medium-high heat. Put the fan on and open a window if possible.

Arrange a piece of plastic wrap large enough to cover the lefse in the center of a clean cloth or old sheet large enough to wrap around the lefse.

Gently place 1 lefse on the dry, hot takke or pan and cook for about 30 seconds or until it begins to bubble on top and turn golden brown on the bottom. Turn the lefse over and cook for about 30 seconds or until golden brown on the other side. Place the cooked lefse on top of the plastic wrap and cover with a second piece of plastic. Fold the sheet over the plastic to keep the lefse soft and moist. Brush any excess flour from the takke or pan so it doesn't burn. Continue making lefse with the remaining dough. Each time you finish a lefse, open the cloth and place it on top of the others, followed by the plastic, and fold the sheet over. When cool, cut into slices and serve immediately or refrigerate for up to 5 days. If freezing, wrap stacks of lefse slices in plastic wrap then cover tightly with foil and freeze for up to 6 months, thawing 30 minutes before serving.

To make a sweet spread, combine sugar and butter (in a 1 to 3 ratio) in a stand mixer fitted with a paddle attachment and beat until completely blended. Evenly spread a good amount of the mixture over a lefse and top with a second one. Cut into individual slices and serve.

Soft Potato Flatbread

POTETLOMPE

Related to lefse, *lompe* is a smaller potato-based soft flatbread. It's often wrapped around hotdogs, but I've found many incredible uses for it. I especially enjoy lompe grilled or fried with just a little oil. It's important to start with smooth mashed potatoes, so use a ricer if you have one.

makes about 15

2 pounds (900 g) starchy potatoes, such as Beate, Kerr's Pink, or russet

1 teaspoon salt

¾ cup (90 g) all-purpose flour, sifted

¾ cup (90 g) rye flour

In a large pot, cover the potatoes with cold salted water and bring to a boil. Lower the heat and simmer for about 20 minutes or until the potatoes are tender when pierced with a knife. Drain the potatoes and cool slightly. Peel the potatoes and, together with the salt, run through a ricer into a large bowl or mash by hand until completely smooth. Mix in the flours; the dough should be soft and pliable but not dry.

Divide the dough into 2-ounce (56 g) balls—there should be about 15.

On a floured surface, use a rolling pin to gently roll out each ball of dough into an 8-inch (20 cm) round, adding more flour as needed. Use a plate or bowl to help shape the rounds into even circles or leave them as is for a more rustic look. Use a soft-bristled brush to brush off any excess flour then use a fork to poke a couple holes in the dough to prevent it from bubbling up while cooking.

Heat a takke over medium-high heat or place a large frying pan directly on the stove over medium-high heat. Put the fan on and open a window if possible. Gently place 1 lompe on the dry, hot takke or pan and cook for about 30 seconds or until golden brown on the bottom. Flip the lompe and cook for 30 seconds until golden brown on the other side. Place the cooked lompe on a plate and cover completely with plastic wrap, followed by a tea towel to keep the lompe soft and moist. Brush any excess flour from the takke or pan so it doesn't burn. Continue making lomper, using the remaining dough and piling them on top of each other under the plastic wrap and tea towel. The lompe can be served immediately or wrapped in plastic and refrigerated for up to 5 days.

Sour Cream Wafers
with Caramelized Sugar

RØMMEBRØD

I first came across these delicate wafers at Uvdalsleiven Tradisjonbakst, a local bakery run by the lovely Hanne. I have taken inspiration from her recipe, which was given to her grandmother by a neighbor many years ago.

Rømmebrød is a thin bread made with sour cream and generously coated with sugar that caramelizes from the heat, creating a lovely pattern of gold and dark brown against creamy white. Typically, rømmebrød is shaped into small rounds and left flat, but Hanne's version is cut into squares and folded over, which adds texture and a beautiful aesthetic. While these wafers are perfect served with whipped cream and fruits or crumbled on top of desserts, they're just as good eaten alone with bare hands. • *makes about 65*

1 cup plus 2 tablespoons (250 g) lightly salted butter, softened

¼ cup plus 2 teaspoons (70 ml) light Norwegian syrup or golden syrup

1¼ cups (300 g) sour cream

4½ cups plus 1 tablespoon (550 g) all-purpose flour, sifted, plus more as needed

Granulated sugar, for sprinkling

In the bowl of a stand mixer fitted with the paddle attachment, beat together the butter and light syrup. Add the sour cream, followed by the flour and beat for about 5 minutes or until the dough is soft but not sticky. Unless the dough is really sticking to your hands, avoid adding more flour. Cover and refrigerate for at least 15 minutes until ready to use.

Tear off a small handful of the dough and place on a floured surface. Using a rolling pin, roll out the dough into a thin rectangle, adding more flour as needed. When you think the dough is as thin as possible, roll it a little more. If the dough is too thick, too many bubbles will form as it cooks and the wafers will be soft rather than crispy. Cut the dough into roughly 6 x 6-inch (15 x 15 cm) squares or similarly sized rectangles. Don't worry if they are not evenly shaped. Continue making rømmebrød with the remaining dough.

Heat a takke to medium-high heat or place a large frying pan directly on the stove over medium-high heat—be careful not to have the heat too high or the sugar may burn rather than caramelize. Put the fan on and open a window if possible.

Butter the takke or pan and add a couple pieces of dough. Sprinkle the dough with sugar and cook for about 1 minute or until bubbles appear on top and the bottoms turn light brown. Flip the squares and sprinkle the other side with sugar. Continue cooking, flipping the dough as needed, for about 5 minutes or until both sides are golden brown and the sugar has melted and caramelized. Transfer to a wire rack to cool as shaped or folded over, like Hanne does, if desired. Using a paper towel, carefully wipe the takke or pan to remove any leftover sugar, which might burn. Continue this process with the remaining dough. Serve the rømmebrød immediately or store in an airtight container at room temperature for up to 3 months.

Griddle Cakes

SVELE

Svele is a traditional flat cake similar to an American pancake, but by no means the same. Flat cakes have a long tradition in Norway—particularly in western Norway—that stretches back to the thirteen hundreds when the daily lives of most Norwegians were marked by poverty. Every ingredient was used to its fullest so as not to be wasted. Sour milk, or *surmelk,* was a common commodity and families mixed leftovers with dry goods for baking. In this recipe, I suggest using kefir—a type of sour milk often used to make svele—but you can substitute it with buttermilk.

While svele, in its many forms, has been popular throughout the centuries, it became closely associated with ferry travel, particularly from the 1970s, as a treat to have alongside a cup of coffee. Served with a slice of *brunost* ("brown cheese") or smear of *smørkrem* ("butter cream"), it remains customary for riders to eat one on board even to this day. It's a tasty indulgence, as travelers begin their journey and waves lap against the side of the boat. • *makes 18*

4 large eggs, at room temperature

½ cup plus 2 tablespoons (125 g) granulated sugar

⅓ cup plus 2 tablespoons (100 g) lightly salted butter, melted

4¼ cups (1 l) kefir

5 cups (600 g) all-purpose flour, sifted

1 teaspoon baking soda

In a large bowl, combine the eggs and sugar and whisk until fluffy. Whisk in the melted butter, followed by the kefir. Combine the flour and baking soda, add to the batter, and stir gently until combined. Let stand for about 20 minutes—the dough will swell.

Heat a takke to medium heat or place a large frying pan directly on the stove over medium heat, and lightly butter.

Ladle some batter onto the hot takke or pan to make several 6-inch (15 cm) round pancakes. Cook for 2 minutes or until bubbles appear on top and the bottoms turn golden brown. Flip the pancakes and cook for 2 minutes more or until the other side is golden brown. Transfer to a plate and keep warm. Continue making pancakes, using the remaining batter and adding butter to the takke or pan as needed.

Serve with brown cheese, jams, sour cream, or butter and sugar. Store the leftovers in a resealable plastic bag or cover with foil and refrigerate for up to 3 days.

Sweet Buns
with Cardamom

BOLLER

The sweet aroma of these buns baking in the oven is utter comfort. *Boller* are Norway's answer to a sweet bread, but instead of just a simple, lightly sweetened yeast dough, these are infused with cardamom. This distinctive and flavorful spice takes baked goods to a whole new level and anyone will tell you cardamom is a key player in Norwegian baking. This recipe is also a great base for different variations. Feel free to fold in some raisins or chocolate, if you desire. • *makes 12*

1¼ cups (300 ml) lukewarm whole milk

2 large eggs, at room temperature

4 cups plus 2 tablespoons (500 g) all-purpose flour, sifted

⅓ cup plus 1 tablespoon (75 g) granulated sugar

1 ounce (25 g) fresh yeast or ⅓ ounce (8.5 g) active dry yeast

1½ teaspoons ground cardamom

¼ teaspoon salt

⅓ cup (75 g) lightly salted butter, chilled, cut into small pieces

1 cup (150 g) raisins, soaked in warm water for at least 1 hour (optional)

In a small bowl, whisk together the lukewarm milk and 1 egg.

In the bowl of a stand mixer fitted with the dough hook attachment, combine the flour, sugar, yeast, cardamom, and salt. Add the milk mixture and knead on low for 8 minutes. Add the butter and knead on medium for about 5 minutes or until the dough is very elastic and somewhat moist. Strain the raisins and knead them into the dough, if using. Transfer the dough to a lightly buttered bowl, cover with a tea towel, and let rise in a warm spot for 1 hour or until doubled in size.

Preheat the oven to 350°F (180°C). Line a baking sheet with parchment paper.

Divide the dough into 12 equal-size pieces and shape into balls. Place the balls of dough on the prepared baking sheet and let rise for 30 minutes.

In a small bowl, whisk the remaining egg. Using a pastry brush, lightly brush the egg on top of the dough. Bake for 12 to 15 minutes or until golden brown. Let cool slightly and serve. Store leftovers in a resealable plastic bag at room temperature for up to 2 days.

Bergen Cinnamon Buns

SKILLINGSBOLLER

These cinnamon buns are pure nostalgia for me. The first time I visited Bergen, my family took me to a bakery in the center of town and bought me my first *skillingsboller*. It was my introduction to Norwegian baked goods and a rite of passage. They're now my favorite and I get one every time I'm in Bergen.

Skillingsboller get their name from an old custom of naming baked goods after their price. They used to cost a skilling apiece though that's certainly not true anymore. It's said that skillingsboller originally contained raisins, but after the war, raisins were difficult to obtain and the buns were sold without them. I like to add rye flour to my version. It gives the buns a bit more texture and depth, which I think complements the sweetness perfectly. • *makes 20*

FOR THE BUNS

⅔ cup (150 g) lightly salted butter

2½ cups (600 ml) milk

5 cups (600 g) all-purpose flour, sifted

2½ cups (300 g) rye flour

¾ cup (150 g) granulated sugar, plus more for sprinkling

2 ounces (50 g) fresh yeast or ⅔ ounces (17 g) active dry yeast

1 teaspoon salt

FOR THE FILLING

¾ cup plus 1 teaspoon (175 g) lightly salted butter, at room temperature

¾ cup plus 2 tablespoons (175 g) granulated sugar

2 tablespoons ground cinnamon

For the buns, in a small saucepan, melt the butter over medium heat. Add the milk and heat until lukewarm. Pour into the bowl of a stand mixer fitted with the dough hook attachment. Add the all-purpose and rye flours, sugar, yeast, and salt. Knead on medium-low for 8 minutes or until soft and elastic. Transfer the dough to a lightly buttered bowl, cover with a tea towel, and let rise in a warm spot for 1 hour or until doubled in size.

For the filling, in a small bowl, combine the butter, sugar, and cinnamon.

On a lightly floured surface, use a rolling pin to roll out the dough into a large rectangle that measures roughly 18 x 24 inches (45 x 60 cm). Using a rubber spatula, spread the filling evenly across the dough all the way to the edges. Roll the long side of the dough around the filling, forming a long, roughly 24-inch (60 cm) log. Using a sharp knife, cut the log into 20 equal-size buns. Divide the buns between the 2 prepared baking sheets, cover with a tea towel, and let rise for 40 minutes.

Preheat the oven to 425°F (220°C) on the convection setting, or 350°F (180°C) on the conventional setting. Line 2 baking sheets with parchment paper.

Bake for 10 minutes or until nicely browned. Transfer to a wire rack to cool. Sprinkle the buns with sugar and serve. Store leftovers in a resealable plastic bag at room temperature for up to 2 days.

Multigrain Bread

GROVBRØD

Bread is a dietary staple in Scandinavia. Norwegians, like most Nordic people, enjoy a range of hearty breads with whole grains, coarse flours, nuts, and seeds. This loaf is my own invention and a cross between Kneipp bread (*kneippbrød*), barley bread (*byggbrød*), and rye bread (*rugbrød*). Kneipp bread is a whole-wheat bread, named after the German doctor Sebastian Kneipp. The recipe made its way to Norway in 1895, when the Hansen Bakery was the first to get a license to bake it and sell it. It's the most commonly consumed bread in the country, which is why I used it as the base for this recipe. My version has a few more ingredients, including oats. It has well-rounded flavor and is oh-so-slightly sweet. The recipe makes two large loaves, so you can freeze one for later or even bake a half batch. • *makes 2 large loaves*

1 cup (120 g) rye flour

1 cup (120 g) barley flour

¾ cup (90 g) quick-cooking oats

2¾ cups plus 1 tablespoon (675 ml) lukewarm water

1¼ cups (300 ml) milk

5½ cups (660 g) all-purpose flour, sifted

3½ cups (420 g) whole-wheat flour

1 ounce (25 g) fresh yeast or ⅓ ounce (8.5 g) active dry yeast

1½ teaspoon salt

3 tablespoons Norwegian dark syrup or light molasses

In a large bowl, combine the rye flour, barley flour, and oats. Add 2 cups (480 ml) of the lukewarm water and let stand for 30 minutes.

In a small saucepan, heat the milk until just warm to the touch.

In the bowl of a stand mixer fitted with the dough hook attachment, combine the white flour, whole-wheat flour, yeast, and salt. Add the warm milk, along with the remaining ¾ cup plus 1 tablespoon (195 ml) lukewarm water and the dark syrup and knead on low speed until combined. Add the oat mixture and continue kneading for 5 minutes or until the dough becomes workable—it should be rather sticky.

On a floured surface, knead the dough a few times then shape into a ball. Transfer to a lightly buttered bowl, cover with a tea towel, and let rise in a warm spot for 45 minutes or until doubled in size.

Preheat the oven to 425°F (220°C). Line a baking sheet with parchment paper.

Divide the dough into two equal parts. On a floured surface, knead each ball of dough a few times then gently form into oval-shaped loaves. Using a sharp knife, make a couple of slits on the top of each loaf. Place the loaves on the prepared baking sheet. Cover with tea towels and let rise for 1 hour.

Dust the tops of the loaves with a little flour and bake for 40 minutes or until golden brown. Transfer to a wire rack to cool. Serve with your favorite toppings and store at room temperature in a resealable plastic bag for up to 2 days. Alternatively, place the cooled loaves in airtight plastic bags and freeze for up to 2 months.

Hearty Crispbread with Honey and Seeds

KNEKKEBRØD

Knekkebrød, also known as "crispbreads" or "breaking breads," are flat and dry, and resemble a cracker. They probably originated in Scandinavia close to five hundred years ago. Some sources say crispbreads were a staple of the Viking diet, because they could be stored for long periods of time. Those crispbreads would have been baked on hot stones; today they're baked in the oven.

Once considered a poor man's food, knekkebrød has become widely popular. There are now numerous variations, including ones that are nutty, herby, salty, and even slightly sweet. Knekkebrød are easy to make, forgiving, and require only a handful of ingredients that can be interchanged depending on what's in your cupboards. All you really need is water and a little imagination. • *makes 30 crispbreads*

1 tablespoon honey

2½ cups (600 ml) warm water

1⅓ cups (135 g) quick-cooking oats

1 cup (135 g) coarse rye flour

½ cup (25 g) wheat bran

½ cup (60 g) pumpkin seeds, roughly chopped

½ cup (80 g) sesame seeds

½ cup (60 g) sunflower seeds

¼ cup (45 g) linseed or flax seeds

1 teaspoon salt

Preheat the oven to 325°F (160°C) on the convection setting, or 350°F (180°C) on conventional setting. Line 2 rimmed baking sheets with parchment paper.

In a medium bowl, combine the honey and warm water and whisk to combine.

In a large mixing bowl, combine the oats, rye flour, wheat bran, pumpkin seeds, sesame seeds, sunflower seeds, linseeds, and salt. Slowly add the honey-infused water, whisking until a wet paste forms. Let stand for 5 minutes so the flours and oats can soak up more of the moisture. Divide the mixture between the prepared baking sheets and use a rubber spatula to spread into a thin, even layer all the way to the edges. Bake for 10 minutes then remove from the oven and carefully cut into 15 rectangles per baking sheet. Return to the oven and bake, alternating the baking sheets twice and occasionally opening the oven door to release steam, for 50 to 60 minutes or until dry and brittle with light browning on the edges. Gently break the crispbreads apart then transfer to a wire rack to cool completely. The crispbreads can be enjoyed immediately or stored in an airtight container at room temperature for up to 2 weeks.

Acknowledgements

To my husband and best friend, Espen, thank you for your endless encouragement, support, patience, and willingness to be my assistant whenever needed. To Oliver, my darling boy, thank you for being my little sous-chef, who is always creating and inspiring me with your ingenuity and generosity.

I owe so much to my incredible family, who has stood by me throughout this project and beyond. Mom and dad, thank you for your immeasurable support, recipe testing, and inspiration. Sarah, thank you for always being there when I need you and for all your help with this book. Kari and Asle, your support has been invaluable. Thank you for guiding me on my culinary journey and for sharing countless recipes. Mike, Katherine, Janne, Neil, Benjamin, Kristian, and Noah, thank you for joining me on this journey from the very beginning, for your constant love, and for being willing tasters. To the rest of my family, spread out all over the world, thank you!

There are so many friends that have gone above and beyond, and deserve so much gratitude. Ingrid and Ann Kristin, thank you for your friendship, love, and constant support. Maj-Lis and Kjell, thank you for opening your kitchen, teaching me, and sharing your recipes. Grethe, thank you for being my *lefse* guru. Kendra, Benita, and Erin, thank you for your assistance and friendship. Liv Jorunn, Ingebjørg, Kari, Lise, Sonja, and Hanne, thank you for not only inviting me into your homes to teach me your recipes, but also for allowing me to share them in this book.

I would also like to thank all my friends and adopted family in Rollag, and the wider Numedal area. You not only supported me in this journey to learn about Norwegian food, but you also fed me, taught me, guided me, and helped me source ingredients and props. There are too many of you to name, but each of you has been instrumental throughout my time here. Thank you!

Of course, all of this would be impossible without the readers of my blog, *North Wild Kitchen*. So many of you have become friends from afar. Thank you for following along, discussing with me, and sharing in my love for this wonderful country and its cuisine.

Finally, I wish to thank my editor, Holly La Due, for seeing the potential in my work and for guiding me and helping me craft this book. I also wish to thank the entire Prestel team for making this book a reality.

Index

Prestel Verlag, Munich • London • New York
A member of Verlagsgruppe Random House GmbH
Neumarkter Strasse 28 • 81673 Munich

In respect to links in the book, Verlagsgruppe Random House
expressly notes that no illegal content was discernible on the linked sites
at the time the links were created. The Publisher has no influence at all
over the current and future design, content or authorship of the linked
sites. For this reason Verlagsgruppe Random House expressly disassociates
itself from all content on linked sites that has been altered since the link
was created and assumes no liability for such content.

Prestel Publishing Ltd.
14-17 Wells Street
London W1T 3PD

Prestel Publishing
900 Broadway, Suite 603
New York, NY 10003

Library of Congress Cataloging-in-Publication Data

Names: Berg, Nevada, author.
Title: North wild kitchen : home cooking from the heart of Norway /
by Nevada Berg.
Description: Munich ; New York : Prestel Verlag, 2018. | Includes index.
Identifiers: LCCN 2018007218 | ISBN 9783791384139 (hardcover)
Subjects: LCSH: Cooking, Norwegian. | Norway--Social life and customs. |
LCGFT: Cookbooks.
Classification: LCC TX722.N6 B47 2018 | DDC 641.59481--dc23
LC record available at https://lccn.loc.gov/201800 7218

A CIP catalogue record for this book is available from the British Library.

Editorial direction: Holly La Due
Design and layout: Jan Derevjanik
Copyediting: Lauren Salkeld
Proofreading: Monica Parcell
Index: Suzanne Foss
Production: Luke Chase

MIX
Paper from
responsible sources
FSC® C008047
FSC
www.fsc.org

Verlagsgruppe Random House FSC® N001967

Printed in China

ISBN 978-3-7913-8413-9

www.prestel.com